A COMPREHENSIVE GUIDE TO PYTHON PROGRAMMING LANGUAGE
PYTHON PROGRAMMING LANGUAGE FOR BEGINNERS

By: Israel Edosomwan

Copyright ©2024 *Israel Edosomwan*
All rights reserved.

Contents

Dedication 7
Acknowledgments 8
About the Author 9
Chapter 1: Introduction 10
    A. Importance Of Python Programming Language: 10
    B. Target Audience - Absolute Beginners: 15
    C. Benefits Of Learning Python: 17
    D. Overview Of The Book Content: 19
Chapter End Exercises 22
    Multiple Choice Questions: 22
    True/False Statements: 24
Coding Practice: 25
Chapter 2: Getting Started with Python 26
    A. Python's Historical Roots And Beginnings: 26
    B. Python Installation And Configuration Process 28
    C. Unveiling Python's IDE Landscape 31
Chapter End Exercise 36
    Multiple Choice Questions: 36
Chapter 3: Python Basics 41
    A. Syntax And Structure Of Python: 41
    B. Introduction To Variables And Data Types: 49
    C. Understanding Operators And Expressions: 54
    D. Decision-Making With If-Else Statements: 57

E. Looping And Iteration With For And While Loops: 61

Chapter End Exercises...67

Multiple Choice Questions: 67

True/False Statements:..69

Coding Practice: 70

Chapter 4: Data Structures And Functions................................71

Manipulating Strings:..71

Working With Lists, Tuples, And Dictionaries:........................76

Understanding Functions And Their Usage: 81

Scope And Parameter Passing In Functions:..........................85

Recursion And Its application 89

Chapter End Exercises 93

Multiple Choice Questions:..93

True/False Statements:..95

Coding Practice 96

Chapter 5: File Handling and Error Handling............................97

A. Reading And Writing Files In Python: 97

B. Exception Handling And Error Types: 101

C. Utilizing Try-Except Blocks: 105

D. Implementing Error Handling In File Operations: 109

Chapter End Exercises 114

Multiple Choice Questions:..114

True/False Statements:..116

Coding Practice 117

Chapter 6: Object-Oriented Programming With Python 119

A. Introduction To Object-Oriented Programming (OOP): ..119

B. Classes And Objects In Python 122

C. Inheritance, Polymorphism, And Encapsulation: 127

D. Working With Modules And Packages: 131

Chapter End Exercises 139

Multiple Choice Questions: 139

True and False: 141

Coding Practice 142

Chapter 7: Advanced Python Concepts 143

A. Regular Expressions And Their Usage: 143

B. Multithreading And Multiprocessing: 148

C. GUI Development With Python Libraries: 152

D. Web Scraping And Data Manipulation: 158

Chapter End Exercise 163

Multiple Choice Questions: 163

True or False: 164

Coding Practice: 165

Chapter 8: Debugging And Testing 166

A. Introduction To Debugging Tools 166

B. Techniques For Efficient Debugging: 171

C. Writing Test Cases And Performing Unit Testing: 175

Chapter End Exercise 180

Multiple Choice Questions: 180

True and False: 181

Coding Practice: 182

Chapter 9: Real-World Applications 183

A. Creating A Web Application With Django: 183

B. Building A Data Analysis Project With Pandas And NumPy
.... 189

C. Developing A Game Using The Pygame Library: 193

Chapter End Exercise 200

Multiple Choice Questions: 200

True and False: 202

Coding Practice: 203

Chapter 10: Best Practices And Further Resources 204

A. Clean Coding Practices: 204

B. Code Optimization Techniques: 209

C. Resources For Further Learning And Community Support:
.... 214

Chapter End Exercise 217

Multiple Choice Questions (MCQs): 217

True/False: 219

Coding Practice: 220

Dedication

To my Mum,

For always being there for me and showing me how to face tough times with a smile. You taught me to never give up and to always look for the good in every situation. This book is for you because you are my hero.

Acknowledgments

I would like to extend my heartfelt appreciation to the editor who meticulously refined the manuscript of this book, ensuring its clarity and coherence. Their dedication to polishing every word has greatly contributed to the quality of the final product.

I also want to express my gratitude to the technical reviewer for their thorough evaluation of the book's content and structure. Their insights and suggestions have been invaluable in ensuring its accuracy and readability.

I am deeply thankful for the support and expertise provided by both individuals throughout the journey of bringing this book to fruition.

About the Author

Israel Edosomwan is a highly skilled DevOps and Cloud Engineer who has developed and launched cloud-based technologies for numerous multinational corporations. He has expertise in DevOps engineering, cloud support, and cloud tools and technologies. He has expedited software development lifecycles and improved teamwork by skillfully integrating DevOps principles. He is an excellent resource for companies looking to embrace cloud computing and DevOps methodologies. As someone who is enthusiastic about lifelong learning, he wrote this book with the goal of imparting his knowledge and experiences.

Chapter 1: Introduction

A. Importance Of Python Programming Language:

Python is a popular programming language that is easy to learn and use. It has gained a lot of popularity in recent years due to its versatility and strong community support. Python is used in a wide range of applications, such as web development, data analysis, machine learning, and scientific computing.

One of the reasons for Python's popularity is its extensive libraries, which provide a wide range of tools and resources for developers. These libraries can be used to perform complex tasks, such as data analysis, without having to write a lot of code from scratch.

Python is also known for its powerful data analysis capabilities. It has a number of built-in tools for working with data, such as NumPy and Pandas, which make it easy to manipulate, clean, and analyze data.

In this section, we will explore the importance of Python programming language in various domains, such as web development, data analysis, and machine learning, backed by illustrations and examples. We will also discuss why Python is a good choice for beginners who are just starting to learn how to code.

1. Versatility:

Python is a computer programming language that can be used for a wide range of tasks. One of the great things about Python is its versatility. It can be used to develop websites, perform complex mathematical calculations, analyze data, automate repetitive tasks, create video games, and even build intelligent systems. One of the advantages of using Python is that it can be applied to many different areas without needing to learn different programming languages. This means that if you learn Python, you can work on various projects across different domains. Whether you're an IT beginner looking to learn how to program or an experienced developer looking to add a new skill to your repertoire, Python is definitely worth considering.

Let's imagine a situation where a developer wants to create a web application. Python frameworks such as Django and Flask offer powerful tools and features for web development. Moreover, Python's extensive libraries make tasks like managing databases (e.g., SQLAlchemy), handling HTTP requests (e.g., requests library), or implementing authentication (e.g., Django-Auth) much easier.

2. Simplicity And Readability:

Python is easy to learn and use for both beginners and experienced programmers. One of the key reasons for its popularity is its emphasis on code readability. This means that the code written in Python is easy to understand, even for someone who is new to programming.

In Python, code is written in a clean and simple syntax, with meaningful indentation. This makes it easier to read and follow the logic of the code. The indentation also reduces the chances of errors and enhances the ease of code maintenance. This means that even if you are not an experienced programmer, you can quickly learn how to write Python code and start creating your own programs.

Python's simplicity also allows developers to focus more on problem-solving rather than dealing with intricate syntax. This makes it a great language for those who want to focus on the logic and functionality of their programs, rather than getting bogged down in the details of the language itself.

Overall, if you are new to programming or looking for an easy-to-learn language, Python is a great choice. Its simplicity and readability make it an ideal language for beginners, while its versatility and power make it a favorite among experienced programmers as well.

Here's an example showcasing Python's simplicity:

```python
def calculate_square(number):
    # This function calculates the square of a number
    return number ** 2

result = calculate_square(5)
print(result) # Output: 25
```

3. Strong Community And Libraries:

Python has a large and active community of experienced developers who actively contribute to its growth. This community provides extensive support, guidance, and resources to its members, including online forums, documentation, and open-source libraries. The availability of numerous libraries in Python promotes faster development and encourages the reuse of existing code.

One such example is the NumPy library, which enables efficient numerical computing with support for multi-dimensional arrays and mathematical functions. Its functionality can be exemplified as follows:

```python
import numpy as np

array1 = np.array([1, 2, 3])

array2 = np.array([4, 5, 6])

result = array1 + array2


print(result) # Output: [5, 7, 9]
```

After importing the NumPy library, two arrays are created and added together element-wise using the "+" operator. The resulting array is then printed to the console.

4. Data Analysis And Machine Learning:

Python has become one of the most widely used programming languages for analyzing data, machine learning, and artificial intelligence. It has some really powerful libraries, such as Pandas, NumPy, Matplotlib, and Scikit-Learn, that provide developers with a wide range of tools for manipulating, analyzing, visualizing, and building machine learning models. These libraries make it easy for developers to tackle complex data tasks quickly and efficiently.

Take the example of the Pandas library, which makes data manipulation tasks a breeze. Imagine having to load a CSV file, filter specific rows, and calculate the average age manually. That would be a daunting and time-consuming task. But with the Pandas library, you can perform these tasks quickly and efficiently, making your data analysis and machine learning projects a lot easier.

```python
import pandas as pd

data = pd.read_csv('data.csv')

# filter data by gender
filtered_data = data[data['gender'] == 'Female']


# calculate the mean age of the filtered data
average_age = filtered_data['age'].mean()
# print the average age
print(average_age)
```

The importance of Python programming language lies in its versatility, simplicity, strong community support, and numerous libraries. It provides excellent tools and resources to tackle diverse challenges efficiently, whether it is web development, scientific computing, or data analysis. Python is an ideal choice for both beginners and experienced developers seeking to enhance their productivity and explore emerging technologies and fields, thanks to its readability and extensive ecosystem.

B. Target Audience - Absolute Beginners:

If you're someone who doesn't have any experience in programming or using Python, you're considered an absolute beginner. You might have become interested in learning Python because you've heard about its popularity and usefulness. Even if you don't have a background in technical fields, you could have different motivations for wanting to learn Python – whether it's personal interest, career growth, or just wanting to use programming to solve problems and automate tasks.

Someone who is just starting to learn how to code might find it challenging to understand the rules and building blocks of the Python programming language. This could be because they are completely new to programming, and Python is the first language they are learning. So, in the beginning, they might have some difficulty grasping fundamental concepts like variables, data types, loops, conditionals, and functions, among others.

If you're an absolute beginner, you might find yourself searching for information online, reading books, watching tutorials, or taking video courses to learn more about it. You might also join communities or forums to ask questions and get more guidance on certain topics. As a beginner, you'll likely need to read, practice, and try out different code examples to get the hang of things. It might take some time, but with persistence and effort, you'll be on your way to mastering Python in no time!

When someone is new to programming, they usually start by getting Python up and running on their computer.

This involves downloading and setting up the tools they need to write and run Python code. There are some programs called IDEs that are great for beginners because they have an easy-to-use interface and can help with fixing errors in the code. Examples of beginner-friendly IDEs include Thonny and PyCharm.

So, for someone who is just starting out with Python programming, it's important to begin with the basics. This means understanding the basic syntax of Python and how to write simple scripts and programs. You'll also need to learn about the different types of data that can be used in Python, such as integers, floats, and strings, as well as the operations that can be performed on them.

Once you have a good grasp of the basics, you can move on to more intermediate concepts. This includes learning about control flow statements like if-else, for, and while loops, as well as collections like lists, tuples, and dictionaries. You'll also need to learn about file handling, functions, and modules, and how to use external libraries to expand your programming capabilities.

As you start learning Python, you might find yourself struggling and making mistakes, but that's completely normal and can actually help you learn better. With hard work, practice, and a problem-solving attitude, you can become proficient in Python and start creating more advanced programs. You can also try building projects, experimenting with different tools, and learning new concepts to expand your knowledge and skills. Just keep exploring and practicing, and you'll be amazed at how much you can achieve!

C. Benefits Of Learning Python:

Python is loved by both beginners and advanced programmers for its user-friendly interface, adaptability, and vast range of libraries. So, let's discuss in detail the various advantages and benefits of learning Python and why it is an excellent choice for anyone who is starting out in the field of programming.

1. Simplicity And Readability:

Python is a programming language that's quite easy to learn because of its clean and simple structure. Its syntax is quite similar to the English language, which makes it easy for beginners to understand and write code elegantly. Unlike other programming languages, Python uses indentation-based blocks instead of complex brackets, which makes the code easier to read and manage.

2. Versatility:

Python is a really useful language that can be put to work in a lot of different ways. You can use it for building websites, analyzing data, creating machine learning models, automating tasks, and more. There are tons of tools and resources available to Python programmers that make it possible to create all sorts of applications for different fields. For example, you might use a library called NumPy to do complex math calculations or a framework like Flask or Django to build a web app. The possibilities are virtually endless!

3. Large And Active Community:

Python has a large and passionate community of developers and enthusiasts. This community is very supportive and provides a wealth of resources and tools for those who are new to the language. They're always ready to help, share knowledge, and collaborate with each other. This helps to keep Python up-to-date and relevant, ensuring that it remains a valuable tool for programmers around the world.

4. Career Opportunities:

If you're looking for a career with a lot of opportunities, learning Python might be a good choice for you. Python is a programming language that can be used in many different ways, and more and more companies are starting to use it for things like analyzing data and automating tasks. As a result, people who are skilled in Python are in high demand. Additionally, Python is also becoming really important in fields like machine learning and artificial intelligence, so if you're interested in those areas, it's definitely worth considering learning Python.

5. Extensive Libraries And Frameworks:

Python has a lot of tools available to help developers create software more easily. These tools can help with things like making graphs and charts to display data or building web applications more quickly. Some popular examples of these tools include Matplotlib, Seaborn, Plotly, Django, and Flask. Using Python and these libraries and frameworks can help make development faster and more efficient.

6. Rapid Prototyping And Development:

Python is great for quickly creating and testing new ideas. It has lots of built-in tools and add-ons that make it easy to create the features you need without spending a lot of time writing code from scratch. Because of this, Python is a popular choice for businesses that want to get their products to market quickly.

7. Educational And Beginner-Friendly:

Python is a great programming language for beginners because it's easy to read and understand. It comes with a lot of helpful resources and guides, making it easy to learn and get started. Even if you've never programmed before, Python can help you build a solid understanding of programming concepts that can be applied to other languages later on. The best part about Python is that it's designed to encourage exploration and creativity, so you can start working on your own projects quickly and easily.

So, in short, learning Python can be extremely beneficial for those who are new to programming. Python is a programming language that is known for its simplicity, versatility, and strong community support. With Python, you can easily access extensive libraries and explore multiple career prospects in fields such as web development, data analysis, machine learning, or automation. It provides a powerful toolset to help you succeed in various domains. So, if you're interested in building innovative applications and exploring the fascinating world of programming, you should definitely give Python a try!

D. Overview Of The Book Content:

We understand that starting a new programming language can be overwhelming, but this book aims to make the learning process as easy and enjoyable as possible.

If you're interested in learning programming, Python is often recommended as a great starting point. It's considered easy to understand and read, making it beginner-friendly.

Unlike other languages that can be confusing due to complex syntax, Python allows aspiring programmers to pick up fundamental concepts with ease. Plus, it's versatile and powerful, making it useful in many areas like web development, data analysis, and even game development.

This book is structured in a way that assumes no prior programming knowledge. Each concept is explained in a clear and concise manner, with examples and exercises that facilitate understanding and hands-on practice. The step-by-step approach ensures a gradual progression from basic concepts to more advanced topics.

This book has been designed to help you learn more effectively. It includes exercises and quizzes at the end of each chapter to test your understanding of the material covered. You'll also find code snippets, and illustrations that make it easier to understand complex concepts. These visual aids will help you learn faster and reinforce your knowledge.

By the time you finish reading this book, even if you have no prior experience in Python programming, you will have a strong understanding of it. You will have gained the knowledge and skills needed to create simple Python programs, work with data structures, manage files, and possibly even create basic web applications, data analysis projects, and games.

Even if you do not have any specific programming goals in mind, learning Python can expand your problem-solving abilities, improve logical thinking, and open up opportunities in various industries. Python is widely used in fields such as web development, scientific computing, data analysis, artificial intelligence, and automation. Having a basic understanding of Python will enable you to explore and navigate these domains with confidence.

This book is a great introduction to Python programming for beginners. It focuses on making the learning process easy and enjoyable. It aims to give you the skills and confidence you need to pursue your programming goals and become a proficient Python developer.

Chapter End Exercises

Multiple Choice Questions:

1. **What is one of the key reasons for Python's popularity?**

    - A. Extensive libraries
    - B. Complex syntax
    - C. Limited community support
    - D. Restriction to specific domains

2. **How does Python contribute to versatility in programming?**

    - A. By having a complex syntax
    - B. By restricting usage to specific domains
    - C. By being applicable to a wide range of tasks
    - D. By limiting the availability of libraries

3. **What does the example using NumPy demonstrate?**

    - A. Data filtering
    - B. Web development
    - C. Numerical computing with arrays
    - D. Video game development

4. **What is emphasized in Python's coding style to enhance readability?**

- A. Random indentation
- B. Complex syntax
- C. Meaningful indentation
- D. Limited libraries

5. **Which library is used for efficient data manipulation tasks in Python?**
    - A. Flask
    - B. SQLAlchemy
    - C. Pandas
    - D. NumPy

True/False Statements:
1. **Python's simplicity allows developers to focus more on syntax intricacies.**
    - A. True
    - B. False

2. **The example showcasing Python's simplicity uses complex logic for square calculation.**
    - A. True
    - B. False

3. **Python's versatility allows it to be used only in web development and data analysis.**
    - A. True
    - B. False

4. **The community and libraries play a significant role in Python's growth and support.**
    - A. True
    - B. False

5. **Panda is a library used for web development in Python.**
    - A. True
    - B. False

Coding Practice:

1. **Write a Python function to calculate the factorial of a given number.**

```
def calculate_factorial(number):
    # Your code here
```

2. **Use the Flask framework to create a simple web application that displays "Hello, Python!" on the homepage.**

```
# Your Flask web application code here
```

3. **Create a NumPy array with values 1 to 5 and perform element-wise multiplication by 2.**

```
import numpy as np

# Your NumPy array manipulation code here
```

4. **Implement a Python class for a basic calculator with methods for addition, subtraction, multiplication, and division.**

```
class Calculator:
    # Your calculator class code here
```

5. **Write a Pandas code snippet to read a CSV file named 'sales_data.csv' and display the first 5 rows.**

```
import pandas as pd

# Your Pandas code for reading and displaying data here
```

Chapter 2: Getting Started with Python

A. Python's Historical Roots And Beginnings:

Exploring the Development Saga Of A User-Friendly Coding Language:

Within this section, we plunge into the extensive history and origins of Python, an adaptable programming language renowned for its straightforwardness and clarity. A comprehensive grasp of Python's evolution, influential contributors, guiding principles in design, and pivotal milestones provides valuable insights into why Python remains a favored choice for both novices and seasoned professionals. Let's traverse the annals of time to unravel the progression of Python and its influence on the programming landscape.

Genesis And Guido Van Rossum's Brainwave:

Guido van Rossum, a Dutch computer scientist, conceived Python in the late 1980s. His vision was to craft a language that prioritized code readability, user-friendliness, and a steadfast commitment to simplicity and lucidity. Drawing inspiration from the ABC programming language, he aspired to create a scripting language that excelled in both system-level programming and rapid prototyping.

Quirks In Python's Nomenclature:

The term "Python" has no correlation with reptiles; rather, it pays homage to the British comedy ensemble Monty Python. As an enthusiast of their humor, van Rossum chose the name to inject an element of amusement into the language. Consequently, Python's libraries and functionalities often incorporate whimsical references to Monty Python sketches and characters.

Early Stages Of Python's Development:

Python's inaugural implementation, coded in C, made its debut in 1991 as Python 0.9.0. It swiftly gained acclaim due to its neat syntax, resilience, and capabilities. Guido van Rossum continued to steer the development and enhancement of Python, assuming the role of its Benevolent Dictator for Life (BDFL).

Core Features And Design Tenets:

The Zen of Python encapsulates the language's guiding philosophy. Advocating simplicity, readability, and practicality, these principles are the backbone of Python's design. Key features, such as dynamic typing, automatic memory management, and an expansive standard library, position it as an ideal entry-level programming language.

Noteworthy Version Upgrades:

Python has undergone multiple version releases, each introducing fresh features and refinements. Standouts include Python 2.0 in 2000, enhancing Unicode support, and Python 3.0 in 2008, ushering in substantial changes and backward incompatibility. The Python 3.x series continues to evolve, with the community actively urging the transition from Python 2.x to 3.x.

Surge In Python's Popularity:

In the last decade, Python's adoption has surged, establishing itself as one of the most favored programming languages globally. Its versatility in realms like web development, data analysis, machine learning, and artificial intelligence significantly contributes to its allure. Python's growth is propelled by a vibrant and engaged community, an extensive library ecosystem, and seamless integration capabilities with other languages.

Influential Python Libraries And Frameworks:

The Python standard library encompasses a diverse array of modules spanning various domains. Additionally, third-party libraries such as NumPy, Pandas, TensorFlow, Django, Flask, and more have transformed specific domains, solidifying Python as an indispensable tool for professionals in science, engineering, and development.

Conclusion:

Grasping the historical backdrop and foundations of Python illuminates the language's progression, design principles, and widespread acclaim. Python's ascent as a user-friendly programming language can be attributed to its simplicity, readability, robust community support, and adaptability. Empowered with this knowledge, readers are poised to explore the boundless possibilities ahead as they embark on their journey to master Python programming.

B. Python Installation And Configuration Process

To initiate your Python programming journey, it is imperative to install Python on your computer and establish the necessary development environment. This section will walk you through the installation and setup process step-by-step, ensuring that you are equipped with everything essential to commence coding in Python successfully.

Selecting The Python Version:

Before commencing the Python installation, it is crucial to determine the version you wish to work with. Presently, Python offers two major versions: Python 2.x and Python 3.x. For beginners, the recommended choice is Python 3.x, given its status as the latest version with enhanced features and support. While Python 2.x is still in use, it reached its end-of-life in 2020, indicating it will no longer receive official updates.

Python Installation Procedure:

Follow these steps to install Python:

a. Visit the official Python website (www.python.org) and navigate to the "Downloads" section.

b. Choose the appropriate installer for your operating system (Windows, macOS, or Linux) and download it.

c. Execute the installer, following the installation wizard, and ensure you select the option to add Python to your system's PATH variable (Windows users).

d. Complete the installation process by accepting the default settings.

Verification Of Installation:

After the installation, it is crucial to confirm the correct installation of Python. Follow these steps:

a. Open the command prompt (Windows) or terminal (macOS/Linux).

b. Type "python" or "python3" (depending on your installation) and press Enter.

c. If the Python interpreter launches, displaying its version, it signifies a successful Python installation.

Establishment Of A Development Environment:

While Python can be executed through the command prompt/terminal, utilizing an Integrated Development Environment (IDE) is recommended for an enhanced coding experience. Some popular choices include:

a. PyCharm: A feature-rich and user-friendly IDE tailored for Python.

b. Visual Studio Code (VS Code): A lightweight and customizable IDE with robust Python support.

c. IDLE: Python's built-in IDE, offering basic features and bundled with the Python installation.

IDE Installation (PyCharm):

Let's guide you through the PyCharm installation as an example:

a. Visit the JetBrains website (www.jetbrains.com/pycharm) and download the free PyCharm Community Edition, suitable for beginners.

b. Execute the installer, following the installation wizard, and select the desired configuration options.

c. Upon completion, launch PyCharm and configure it by specifying the path to your Python interpreter (usually located in the Python installation directory).

Crafting And Executing Your Inaugural Python Script:

To validate the functionality of your Python installation and IDE setup, let's compose a straightforward "Hello, World!" program:

a. Launch your preferred IDE and initiate a new Python file.

b. Input the subsequent code:

print("Hello, World!")

c. Save the file with a .py extension (e.g., hello_world.py).

d. Execute the program, and you should observe the output "Hello, World!" printed in the console.

Conclusion:

In this section, you've acquired the know-how to install Python, confirm the installation, establish a development environment using an IDE, and execute your inaugural Python program. By adhering to these steps, you are now equipped with the essentials to embark on your journey into the realm of Python programming.

C. Unveiling Python's IDE Landscape

Python stands out as a sought-after programming language renowned for its simplicity and clarity, particularly suitable for beginners. To initiate Python coding, you must delve into the realm of a development environment, commonly known as an Integrated Development Environment (IDE). This section will navigate you through the basics of setting up and leveraging a Python IDE for scripting and executing Python programs.

Defining An IDE:

An IDE is a software application that furnishes comprehensive tools to aid programmers in creating, editing, and executing their code. It typically encompasses a text editor, a compiler, or an interpreter, along with additional features like code completion, debugging tools, and integration with version control.

Opting For The Appropriate IDE:

Several Python IDEs cater to diverse needs and preferences. Here are a few popular choices:

PyCharm: A robust IDE crafted by JetBrains featuring intelligent code completion, debugging capabilities, and integrated version control.

Visual Studio Code (VS Code): A lightweight and customizable IDE with stellar Python language support and an extensive ecosystem of extensions.

IDLE: Python's default IDE, straightforward and lightweight, suitable for beginners but lacking advanced features.

For this section, our focus will be on IDLE, given its inclusion with the Python installation, making it readily accessible to beginners.

Python And IDLE Installation:

Before we proceed, ensure Python is installed on your system. Visit python.org, download the latest version compatible with your operating system, and during installation, ensure the IDLE option is selected.

Initiating IDLE:

Once installed, access IDLE by searching for it in your operating system's applications menu or by running the "IDLE" executable. Upon launching IDLE, you'll encounter the Python Shell, a prompt facilitating the interactive entry and execution of Python code.

Features And Functions Of IDLE:

IDLE provides various features to enhance your Python programming experience. Let's explore key components:

Text Editor: IDLE incorporates a basic text editor, offering features such as syntax highlighting, indentation guides, and automatic indentation for crafting clean and readable code.

Python Shell: The Python Shell in IDLE enables interactive coding, allowing the execution of individual lines or code blocks with immediate output. This feature is particularly useful for testing small code snippets before integration into larger programs.

Debugger: IDLE includes a debugger for identifying and rectifying errors in your code. It facilitates setting breakpoints, stepping through code execution, and inspecting variables to comprehend the program's behavior.

Python Documentation: IDLE integrates Python's official documentation, providing swift access to libraries, modules, functions, and their usage. This built-in reference proves invaluable for exploring Python's extensive capabilities.

Composing Your Inceptive Python Program In IDLE:

Let's draft a basic "Hello, World!" program using IDLE:

Open IDLE, and a new untitled window will materialize.

In this window, input the following code:

print("Hello, World!")

Save the file with a .py extension on your system, such as "helloworld.py."

To execute the program, navigate to the "Run" menu, select "Run Module," or use the F5 key (on Windows/Linux) or Fn + F5 (on Mac).

The Python Shell will showcase the output: "Hello, World!"

Exploring Additional IDE Options:

While IDLE provides a simple and beginner-friendly environment, you may want to delve into more feature-rich IDEs like PyCharm or Visual Studio Code as you progress in your Python journey. These IDEs offer advanced functionalities such as code analysis, integrated terminal, source control integration, and plugin support, augmenting productivity and the overall programming experience.

Conclusion:

In this section, we introduced you to the Python development environment (IDE). We explored the concept of IDEs, emphasized the importance of selecting the right IDE, and delved into the installation and basic utilization of IDLE, Python's default IDE. We also dissected essential features of IDLE, including the text editor, Python Shell, debugger, and built-in documentation. Lastly, we guided you through composing a simple "Hello, World!" program in IDLE. Armed with this foundation, you are now prepared to immerse yourself in Python programming using an IDE of your choice.

Chapter End Exercise

Multiple Choice Questions:

1. Python 3.0, released in 2008, brought:

    a. Backward compatibility with Python 2.x
    b. Substantial changes and backward incompatibility
    c. Enhanced support for Unicode
    d. Only bug fixes

2. Why is it crucial to verify the Python installation after completion?

    e. To impress colleagues
    f. To ensure the correct installation
    g. To test Python's backward compatibility
    h. To demonstrate Python's popularity

3. Why is IDLE recommended for beginners in this section?

    i. It has advanced features for experienced programmers
    j. It is lightweight and suitable for beginners
    k. It includes built-in support for Monty Python references
    l. It is the only IDE compatible with Python 3.x

4. What is the purpose of the Python Shell in IDLE?

    m. It serves as a habitat for programming snakes
    n. It allows execution of individual lines or code blocks interactively
    o. It is a decorative element with Python-themed animations
    p. It stores Monty Python scripts for reference

5. **What is the advantage of exploring more feature-rich IDEs like PyCharm or Visual Studio Code?**

    q. They offer Python-themed backgrounds
    r. They provide advanced functionalities and support for Python development
    s. They include built-in Monty Python game modules
    t. They translate code into Monty Python quotes automatically

True/False Statements:

1. Python 2.x is the recommended version for beginners due to its extensive library support.

    - A. True
    - B. False

2. Guido van Rossum, the creator of Python, chose the name "Python" in reference to his fascination with reptiles.

    - A. True
    - B. False

3. Python 3.0, released in 2008, maintained backward compatibility with the previous Python 2.x versions

    - A. True
    - B. False

4. It is optional to add Python to the system's PATH variable during installation, and it does not impact the functionality of Python.

    - A. True
    - B. False

5. The Python standard library encompasses only core modules, and external third-party libraries do not contribute to Python's versatility

- .A. True
- B. False

Coding Practice:

1. **Write a Python script that prints your name and a greeting message to the console.**

Print a greeting message using the print function with your name and a message.

2. **Create a Python program that calculates the sum of the first 10 positive integers.**

Use the formula for the sum of the first n positive integers: (n * (n + 1)) / 2.

3. **Develop a Python script that defines a list of your favorite programming languages and prints each language in the list.**

Define a list of programming languages and iterate through it to print each language using a loop.

4. **Write a Python function that takes two parameters (width and height) and calculates the area of a rectangle.**

Create a function with parameters width and height and return the product of the two values for the area.

5. **Implement a Python program that prompts the user to enter their age and prints a message based on whether they are considered minor or an adult.**

Use an if-else statement to check if the entered age is below or equal to 18 and print appropriate messages.

Chapter 3: Python Basics

A. Syntax And Structure Of Python:

In this section, we will explore the syntax and structure of the Python programming language. Syntax essentially comprises a set of guidelines that dictate how a program should be written, while structure relates to the way in which statements, functions, and blocks are organized within a program. For beginners, it is pivotal to comprehend the syntax and structure of Python in order to write code that is both efficient and free of errors. The objective of this section is to provide a comprehensive overview of the fundamental aspects of Python syntax and the manner in which they contribute to the overall structure of a Python program.

1. Comments:

In Python, the pound sign (#) is used to indicate a comment. Comments are ignored by the interpreter and are used to add information or explanations to the code for human readers. In the following code snippet, the line `# This is a comment` is a comment that does not affect the execution of the code.

```python
# This is a comment
```

2. Statements And Lines:

Python code is composed of statements, which are individual instructions. Each statement is typically written on a separate line. Python allows multiple statements on a single line, separated by semicolons. Here's an example:

```python
print("Hello,")
print("world!")
```

The first line uses the `print` function to display the text "Hello" on the console or terminal. The second line uses the same function to display the text "world!" on a new line.

When executed, the output would be:

```
Hello,
world!
```

3. Blocks And Indentation:

In Python, blocks of code are identified by their indentation level rather than by the use of braces or parentheses. The indentation serves as a determining factor for grouping and execution order of statements. It is generally recommended to use four spaces for indentation. Here is an example:

```python
if True:
    print("This statement is inside the block.")
    print("These statements are also inside the block.")
```

```
print("This statement is outside the block.")
```

This is an example of a conditional statement in Python. The `if` statement checks if the condition inside the parentheses is True. In this case, it is always True because the condition is the boolean value `True.`

The code inside the block is executed only when the condition is True. In this case, the three `print` statements are inside the block, so they will be executed. The first two statements will be printed because they are inside the block. The third `print` statement is outside the block, so it will be executed regardless of whether the condition is True or False.

If the condition was False, the statements inside the block would not be executed, and only the third `print` statement would be executed.

4. Variables:

Variables are used to store data and give them meaningful names. In Python, you can assign values to variables using the `=` operator. Unlike some languages, Python does not require explicit variable type declaration. Here's an example:

```python
x = 10

message = "Hello, World!"
```

The first line, `x = 10` initializes a variable named `x` with a value of 10. In Python, you don't need to declare a variable type explicitly. Instead, Python infers the type of the variable based on the value assigned to it.

The second line `message = "Hello, World!"` initializes a variable named `message` with a string value of "Hello, World!". A string is a sequence of characters enclosed in single or double quotes.

So, in summary, this code creates two variables named `x` and `message` and assigns them the values of 10 and "Hello, World!" respectively.

5. Data Types:

Python supports various data types, including numbers, strings, lists, tuples, dictionaries, and more. Each data type has specific properties and methods for performing operations. Here are a few examples:

```python
# Numbers

x = 10

y = 3.14
```

The variables `x` and `y` are assigned the values `10` and `3.14`, respectively, which are examples of numeric data types in Python.

```
# Strings

name = "John"

message = "Hello, " + name
```

The variables `name` and `message` are assigned the values `"John"` and `"Hello, John"`, respectively, which are examples of string data types in Python.

Lists

fruits = ["apple", "banana", "orange"]

The variable `fruits` is assigned a list of strings `["apple", "banana", "orange"]`, which is an example of a list data type in Python. A list is an ordered collection of elements that can be of different data types.

Tuples

point = (3, 4)

The variable `point` is assigned a tuple `(3, 4)`, which is an example of a tuple data type in Python. A tuple is an ordered collection of elements that are immutable, meaning that they cannot be modified once they are created.

Dictionaries

student = {"name": "John", "age": 20}

```

The variable `student` is assigned a dictionary `{"name": "John", "age": 20}`, which is an example of a dictionary data type in Python. A dictionary is an unordered collection of key-value pairs, where each key is associated with a value.

**6. Operators:**

Python provides a wide range of operators for performing arithmetic, comparison, and logical operations.
```

These operators can be used with variables or literal values. Here are some commonly used operators:

```python
# Arithmetic Operators

x = 10 + 5

y = 10 / 3
```

These are used for performing mathematical operations such as addition, subtraction, multiplication, and division. In the given code snippet, `x` is assigned the value of `10 + 5`, which is `15`, and `y` is assigned the value of `10 / 3`, which is approximately `3.33`.

```python
# Comparison Operators

is_equal = x == y

is_greater = x > y
```

These are used to compare two values and return a Boolean value (`True` or `False`) based on the comparison. In the given code snippet, `is_equal` is assigned the value of `x == y`, which compares the values of `x` and `y` and returns `False` because `x` is not equal to `y`. Similarly, `is_greater` is assigned the value of `x > y`, which compares `x` and `y` and returns `True` because `x` is greater than `y`.

```python
# Logical Operators

is_both_true = True and False

is_either_true = True or False
```

These are used to combine multiple Boolean values and return a single Boolean value. In the given code snippet, `is_both_true` is assigned the value of `True and False`, which returns `False` because both operands are not `True`. On the other hand, `is_either_true` is assigned the value of `True or False`, which returns `True` because at least one operand is `True`.

7. Control Flow:

Python offers various control flow statements, such as if-else statements, loops, and function definitions, to control the execution flow of a program. These statements allow programmers to make decisions and repeat certain actions based on conditions. Here are a few examples:

```python
# if-else statement
if x > 10:
    print("x is greater than 10")
else:
    print("x is less than or equal to 10")

# for loop
for fruit in fruits:
    print(fruit)

# while loop
i = 0
while i < 5:
```

```
print(i)

i += 1

# function definition

def greet(name):

    print("Hello, " + name)

greet("John") # Output: Hello, John
```
```

The code snippet is an example of basic Python syntax for control structures, loops, and function definition.

The first block of code shows an if-else statement. This is a conditional statement in Python that allows the program to execute different code blocks depending on whether the condition is true or false. In this case, if the variable `x` is greater than 10, the program will print "x is greater than 10". Otherwise, it will print "x is less than or equal to 10".

The second block is an example of a for loop. A for loop is used to iterate over a sequence, in this case, a list of fruits. For each fruit in the list, the program will print the name of the fruit.

The third block is a while loop. A while loop allows the program to iterate over a block of code as long as the condition is true. In this case, the program will print the value of variable `i` as long as `i` is less than 5. The value of `i` is incremented by 1 after each iteration using the statement `i += 1`.

The fourth block is a function definition. A function is a block of code that performs a specific task. In this case, the
```

`greet()` function takes a name as an argument and prints the string "Hello" followed by the name. The function is called with the argument "John", so the program will print "Hello, John".

Conclusion

In this section, we have covered the essential aspects of Python's syntax and structure. We discussed how comments, statements, blocks, variables, data types, operators, and control flow statements are used in Python programming. Understanding these fundamental concepts will help beginners write clear, concise, and effective Python code. It is crucial to practice and explore more examples to gain a strong grasp of Python's syntax and structure.

B. Introduction To Variables And Data Types:

In this section, we will explore one of the fundamental concepts in programming - variables and data types. Understanding these concepts is crucial for any beginner learning the Python programming language.

1. What Are Variables?

Variables are like containers that hold values. These values can be of different data types, such as numbers, text, boolean (True or False), or more complex types like lists and dictionaries. Variables are used to store and manipulate data during program execution.

2. Declaring Variables

In Python, you don't need to declare variables with their types explicitly. You can simply assign a value to a variable using the assignment operator (=). For example:

```
```

```
x = 10

name = "John"

is_verified = True
```

The first line, `x = 10`, assigns the value `10` to the variable `x`. Variables are used to store data in a program.

The second line, `name = "John"` assigns the string value `"John"` to the variable `name`. In Python, strings are used to represent text.

The third line, `is_verified = True` assigns the Boolean value `True` to the variable `is_verified`. Boolean values are used to represent the truth values `True` and `False`.

Overall, this code snippet defines three variables: `x`, `name`, and `is_verified`, and assigns values to them.

3. Data Types In Python:

Python has several built-in data types, including:

Numeric types: integers (int) and floating-point numbers (float)

- Text type: strings (str)
- Boolean type: True or False (bool)
- Sequence types: lists, tuples, and ranges
- Mapping type: dictionary (dict)
- Set types: set and frozen set
- NoneType: represents the absence of a value (None)

4. Numeric Types:

Numeric types are used to represent numbers. Python provides two numeric types:

- Integers (int): These are whole numbers without any decimals.

Example: `x = 10`

- Floating-point numbers (float): These are numbers with decimal points.

Example: `y = 3.14`

5. Strings:

Strings are used to represent text or characters in Python. They can be enclosed in single (') or double ("") quotes. Examples:

```
name = "Alice"

message = 'Hello, world!'
```

Strings are highly versatile and can be manipulated in various ways, such as concatenation, slicing, and formatting.

6. Booleans:

Boolean type represents the truth values, True or False. It is commonly used in conditions and logical operations. For example:

```
```

```
is_raining = True

has_money = False
```

7. Lists

A list is an ordered collection of items enclosed in square brackets ([])and separated by commas. Each item in a list can be of any data type.

```
numbers = [1, 2, 3, 4, 5]

names = ["Alice", "Bob", "Charlie"]
```

Lists can be modified by adding, removing, or changing elements.

8. Dictionaries:

A dictionary is an unordered collection of key-value pairs enclosed in curly braces ({}). Each key is unique, and its corresponding value can be any data type.

```
student = {"name": "Alice", "age": 20, "grade": "A"}
```

Dictionaries are useful for storing and retrieving data based on a specific key.

9. NoneType

NoneType represents the absence of a value. It is often used to indicate that a variable has no value assigned to it. For example:

```
result = None
```

NoneType can be helpful in initializing variables or as a placeholder value.

In conclusion, variables and data types are essential building blocks for programming in Python. By understanding different data types and their usage, you can store and manipulate various kinds of information within your programs. Remember to choose appropriate variable names, as they make your code more readable and self-explanatory.

Illustration:

Imagine a storage room with different types of containers representing data types (e.g., boxes for integers, bottles for floats, etc.). Each container (variable) can hold a specific value, and you can access, modify, or replace the contents as needed.

Example:

```
# Calculate the area of a rectangle
length = 5
width = 3
```

```
area = length * width

print(area)  # Output: 15
```
```

In the above example, we calculate the area of a rectangle by multiplying the length and width variables and assigning the result to the area variable. Finally, we print the result using the print function.

Remember, mastering variables and data types is essential for building more complex programs in Python, and it's a foundation for further learning in the language.

### C. Understanding Operators And Expressions:

In Python programming language, operators are special symbols that perform specific operations on operands to produce a result. Expressions, on the other hand, are combinations of operators, variables, and constants that evaluate a value. Understanding the different types of operators and expressions in Python is crucial for any beginner programmer. In this section, we will explore various operators and expressions in Python with detailed explanations, illustrations, and examples.

#### 1. Arithmetic Operators:

Arithmetic operators are used to perform basic mathematical operations. Python provides several arithmetic operators, including addition (+), subtraction (-), multiplication (*), division (/), modulo (%), and exponentiation (**). Let's see how these operators work with examples and illustrations.

**Illustration:**
```

Consider two variables, a = 10 and b = 3.

Examples:

- 1. Addition: a + b = 10 + 3 = 13
- 2. Subtraction: a - b = 10 - 3 = 7
- 3. Multiplication: a * b = 10 * 3 = 30
- 4. Division: a / b = 10 / 3 = 3.33333 (floating-point division)
- 5. Modulus: a % b = 10 % 3 = 1 (remainder after division)
- 6. Exponentiation: a ** b = 10 ** 3 = 1000 (10 raised to the power of 3)

2. Comparison Operators:

Comparison operators are used to compare values and return a Boolean result (True or False). Python provides various comparison operators, including equal to (==), not equal to (!=), greater than (>), less than (<), greater than or equal to (>=), and less than or equal to (<=). Let's understand these operators with examples and illustrations.

Illustration:

Consider two variables, x = 5 and y = 7.

Examples:

- 1. Equal to: x == y -> False
- 2. Not equal to: x != y -> True
- 3. Greater than: x > y -> False
- 4. Less than: x < y -> True
- 5. Greater than or equal to: x >= y -> False
- 6. Less than or equal to: x <= y -> True

3. Logical Operators:

Logical operators are used to combine Boolean values and perform logical operations. Python provides logical operators, including and, or, and not. These operators are often used in control flow and conditional statements. Let's explore the logical operators with examples and illustrations.

Illustration:

Consider two Boolean values, p = True and q = False.

Examples:

- 1. and operator: p and q -> False
- 2. or operator: p or q -> True
- 3. not operator: not p -> False, not q -> True

These logical operators help us make decisions based on multiple conditions and control the flow of our program.

4. Assignment Operators:

Assignment operators are used to assign values to variables. Python provides various assignment operators, including =, +=, -=, *=, /=, %=, **=, and //= to perform complex assignments. Let's understand these operators with examples and illustrations.

Illustration:

Consider a variable, z = 5.

Examples:

- 1. Simple assignment: z = 5

- 2. Addition assignment: z += 2 -> z = z + 2 -> z = 7
- 3. Subtraction assignment: z -= 2 -> z = z - 2 -> z = 3
- 4. Multiplication assignment: z *= 2 -> z = z * 2 -> z = 10
- 5. Division assignment: z /= 2 -> z = z / 2 -> z = 2.5
- 6. Modulus assignment: z %= 2 -> z = z % 2 -> z = 1
- 7. Exponentiation assignment: z **= 2 -> z = z ** 2 -> z = 25
- 8. Floor division assignment: z //= 2 -> z = z // 2 -> z = 2

These assignment operators help in performing operations and assigning the result back to the variable.

Conclusion

In this section, we have covered the fundamental concepts of operators and expressions in Python programming. Understanding how operators work and how to express operations using expressions is crucial for writing effective and efficient Python programs. By grasping the concepts of arithmetic, comparison, logical, and assignment operators, beginners can build a solid foundation in Python programming. Practice these concepts with the provided examples and illustrations to enhance your understanding and proficiency.

D. Decision-Making With If-Else Statements:

In Python programming, decision-making is a crucial concept that enables the execution of specific code blocks based on particular conditions. One of the most commonly used decision-making structures is the if-else statement.

This section will provide a comprehensive explanation of if-else statements, including their syntax, purpose, and practical examples with illustrations.

1. Syntax Of If-Else Statements:

The basic syntax for an if-else statement in Python is as follows:

```python
if condition:
    # Block of code to be executed if condition is True
else:
    # Block of code to be executed if condition is False
```

The `if` statement is used to check if a certain condition is true or false. If the condition is true, the code inside the `if` block will be executed. Otherwise, the code inside the `else` block will be executed.

Here, the `condition` is the expression that is evaluated to be true or false. If the `condition` is true, the block of code under the `if` statement will be executed, and if it's false, the block of code under the `else` statement will be executed.

Note that in Python, indentation is very important. The code under the `if` and `else` statements should be indented to show that it's a part of the block of code to be executed if the condition is true or false, respectively.

2. Purpose Of If-Else Statements:

The primary purpose of if-else statements is to control the flow of execution in a program based on certain conditions. With if-else statements, you can instruct the program to take different paths or perform specific actions depending on whether a condition evaluates to True or False.

3. How If-Else Statements Work:

When an if-else statement is encountered, the condition is evaluated. If the condition is True, the code within the if block is executed. If the condition is False, the code within the else block is executed (if present). Only one of the two blocks will be executed, never both.

4. Examples And illustrations:

Example 1: Checking If A Number Is Positive Or Negative:

```python
num = -7

if num >= 0:

    print("The number is positive or zero.")

else:


    print("The number is negative.")
```

Illustration

Assuming the value of 'num' is -7, the condition 'num >= 0' evaluates to False, so the code within the else block will be executed. Consequently, the output will be `"The number is negative."`

Example 2: Determining If A Student Passed Or Failed An Exam:

```python
score = 80

if score >= 70:

    print("Congratulations! You passed the exam.")

else:

    print("Sorry, you failed the exam.")
```

Illustration:

If the 'score' variable holds the value 80, the condition 'score >= 70' evaluates to True, and the code within the if block will be executed. Thus, the output will be `"Congratulations! You passed the exam."`

Example 3: Categorizing Numbers Into Odd Or Even:

```python
number = 9

if number % 2 == 0:

    print("The number is even.")
```

```
else:
    print("The number is odd.")
```

Illustration:

For the variable 'number' holding the value 9, the condition 'number % 2 == 0' evaluates to False. Therefore, the code within the else block gets executed, resulting in the output `"The number is odd."`

Conclusion:

If-else statements are a fundamental aspect of Python programming that enables developers to make decisions based on specific conditions. This section offers a comprehensive explanation of if-else statements, their syntax, and purpose and provides illustrative examples. These examples are particularly useful for beginners as they offer a clear understanding of how if-else statements work and how to apply them in their own Python programs.

E. Looping And Iteration With For And While Loops:

Repetition of code is an essential part of programming, and loops provide us with a way to achieve this. Python offers two types of loops, namely for loops and while loops, which we can use to repeat a block of code several times. In this section, we will discuss both loop types, getting familiar with their syntax and discovering how to use them efficiently in different situations.

1. The for Loop:

The for loop is commonly used when we have a predetermined number of iterations or when we want to iterate over a sequence, such as a list or a string. Let's dive into the syntax and usage of the for loop:

Syntax:

```
for variable in iterable:
    # code block
```

Explanation:

The `variable` (can be named anything) is used to capture each item or element during each iteration.

The `iterable` is the sequence or collection we want to iterate over.

The code block executes once for every item in the iterable.

Example:

```python
fruits = ["apple", "banana", "orange"]
for fruit in fruits:
    print(fruit)
```

Illustration:

```
Iteration 1: fruit = "apple"
Output: "apple"
Iteration 2: fruit = "banana"
Output: "banana"
Iteration 3: fruit = "orange"
Output: "orange"
```

2. The while Loop:

The while loop is suitable when we have an unknown number of iterations and want to keep executing the loop until a specific condition is met. Let's explore the syntax and usage of the while loop:

Syntax:

```
while condition:
    # code block
```

Explanation:

The `condition` is a Boolean expression that is evaluated before each iteration. If it is True, the loop continues; otherwise, it terminates.

The code block inside the loop executes as long as the condition is True.

Example:

```python
count = 1

while count <= 5:

    print("Count:", count)

    count += 1
```

Illustration:

```

Iteration 1: count = 1

Output: "Count: 1"

Iteration 2: count = 2

Output: "Count: 2"

Iteration 3: count = 3

Output: "Count: 3"

Iteration 4: count = 4

Output: "Count: 4"


Iteration 5: count = 5
```

Output: "Count: 5"

```

### 3. Loop Control Statements:

Python provides additional loop control statements that allow us to manipulate the flow of our loops. Here are some commonly used control statements:

- ❖ `break`: Terminates the loop prematurely, regardless of the loop's condition, and transfers control to the next statement after the loop.

    **Example:**

    ```python
    fruits = ["apple", "banana", "orange"]
    for fruit in fruits:
        if fruit == "banana":
            break
        print(fruit)
    ```

    Output: "apple"

- ❖ `Continue`: Skips the current iteration and moves to the next iteration of the loop.

    Example:

    ```python
    fruits = ["apple", "banana", "orange"]

```
for fruit in fruits:

    if fruit == "banana":

        continue

    print(fruit)
```

Output: "apple", "orange"

These control statements allow us to have precise control over the execution of our loops, enhancing their functionality.

Conclusion

Loops are invaluable tools in programming, and mastering for and while loops is essential for any Python developer. With the for loop, we can iterate over a sequence or collection, while the while loop allows us to repeat a code block until a specific condition is met. Understanding the syntax and proper usage of these loops, along with loop control statements, will greatly empower you to write efficient and dynamic programs.

Remember, practice is key! Experiment with loop examples and explore more complex scenarios to enhance your proficiency in loop-based programming.

Chapter End Exercises

Multiple Choice Questions:

1. What symbol is used to indicate a comment in Python?

    - A) //
    - B) #
    - C) /
    - D) <!-- -->

2. How are blocks of code identified in Python?

    - A) By using braces {}
    - B) By using parentheses ()
    - C) By indentation
    - D) By using square brackets []

3. Which of the following statements is true about Python variables?

    - A) Python requires explicit variable type declaration.
    - B) Variables in Python cannot be reassigned once a value is assigned.
    - C) Variable names must start with a capital letter.
    - D) Python infers the type of the variable based on the value assigned to it.

4. Which data type represents an ordered collection of elements that are immutable?

- A) List
- B) Tuple
- C) Dictionary
- D) Set

5. What is the output of the following code snippet?

$$x = 10$$

$$y = 3$$

result = x / y

print(result)

- A) 3.3333333333333335
- B) 3.0
- C) 3
- D) Error

True/False Statements:
1. In Python, comments are executed along with the code.

2. Python variables must be explicitly declared with their data type.

3. The condition in an if-else statement must always evaluate to a boolean value.

4. A tuple in Python is mutable, meaning its elements can be changed after creation.

5. The break statement in Python terminates the entire program execution.

Coding Practice:

Write a Python program to calculate the factorial of a given number using a recursive function. Test your program with a few different numbers to verify its correctness.

```python
def calculate_factorial(number):
    if number == 0 or number == 1:
        return 1
    else:
        return number * calculate_factorial(number - 1)

# Test cases
print(calculate_factorial(5))  # Output: 120
print(calculate_factorial(0))  # Output: 1
print(calculate_factorial(3))  # Output: 6
```

This program defines a recursive function **calculate_factorial** to compute the factorial of a given number. The function returns 1 when the input number is 0 or 1 (base cases), and otherwise recursively calls itself with **number - 1** until reaching the base cases.

Chapter 4: Data Structures And Functions
Manipulating Strings:
Introduction:

Strings are an essential data type in Python, serving as a means of representing and manipulating textual information. In this section, we will dive into the world of string manipulation, exploring various techniques and functions available in Python. By the end, you will have a solid understanding of how to work with strings effectively, enabling you to manipulate and transform text data to meet your programming needs.

Section 1: Accessing Characters In A String:

Illustration:

Below is an illustration showcasing a string with its characters indexed:

String: "Hello, World!" Index: 0123456789101112

0:H	1:e	2:l	3:l	4:o	5:,	6:
7:W	8:o	9:r	10:l	11:d	12: !	

In the above example, each character in the string "Hello, World!" is indexed starting from 0.

This means that 'H' is at index 0, 'e' is at index 1, 'l' is at index 2, and so on.

This indexing allows us to easily access individual characters within the string for various operations.

In this section, we will learn how to access individual characters within a string, which is crucial for performing various operations such as extraction, manipulation, and transformation.

1.1 Indexing:

- Python uses zero-based indexing to access characters in a string.

- Example: `message = "Hello, World!"` -> `message[0]` would return "H".

1.2 Negative Indexing:

- We can use negative indices to access characters from the end of a string.

- Example: `message[-1]` would return "!".

Section 2: Manipulating Strings

Illustration: Below is an illustration showcasing various operations on strings:

Original String: "Hello, World!"

1. Concatenation: String 1: "Hello, " String 2: "World!" Result: "Hello, World!"
2. Substring Extraction: Original String: "Hello, World!" Substring (index 3 to 7): "lo, W"
3. String Length: Original String: "Hello, World!" Length: 13
4. Case Conversion: Original String: "Hello, World!" Uppercase: "HELLO, WORLD!" Lowercase: "hello, world!"
5. Reversal: Original String: "Hello, World!" Reversed String: "!dlroW ,olleH"

6. String Replacement: Original String: "Hello, World!" Replace "World" with "Universe": Result: "Hello, Universe!"

These operations demonstrate how strings can be manipulated and transformed to suit different requirements, such as concatenation, extraction, case conversion, reversal, and replacement.

In this section, we will explore different operations that can be performed on strings, allowing us to manipulate and transform them according to our requirements.

2.1 **Concatenation**:

- The addition operator (+) allows us to combine two or more strings together.

- Example: `str1 = "Hello"`, `str2 = " World"`, `result = str1 + str2` -> `result` would be "Hello World".

2.2 String Repetition:

- We can repeat a string multiple times using the multiplication operator (*).

- Example: `str1 = "Python!"`, `result = str1 * 3` -> `result` would be "Python!Python!Python!".

2.3 String Length:

- The `len()` function returns the length of a string.

- Example: `message = "Good morning!"`, `length = len(message)` -> `length` would be 13.

2.4 String Slicing:

- Slicing allows us to extract a portion of a string based on specified indices. message = "Python programming"

sub_string = message[7:18]

print(sub_string)

- Example: `message = "Python programming"`, `sub_string = message[7:18]` -> `sub_string` would be "programming".

Section 3: Modifying Strings

Illustration: Here's an illustration showcasing modifying string characters:

Original String: "Hello, World!"

1. Replacing Characters: Original String: "Hello, World!" Replace 'o' with 'x': Result: "Hellx, Wxrld!"

2. Removing Characters: Original String: "Hello, World!" Remove 'l': Result: "Heo, Word!"

3. Changing Case: Original String: "Hello, World!" Change to uppercase: Result: "HELLO, WORLD!" Change to lowercase: Result: "hello, world!"

4. Splitting Strings: Original String: "Hello, World!" Split by comma: Result: ["Hello", " World!"] Split by space: Result: ["Hello,", "World!"]

These techniques demonstrate various ways to modify strings by replacing or removing characters, changing case, and splitting strings according to different requirements.

In this section, we will explore techniques to modify strings by replacing or removing characters, changing case, or splitting strings.

3.1 Changing Case:

- We can convert strings to lowercase or uppercase using the `lower()` and `upper()` functions, respectively.

- Example:

```
message = "Hello, World!"
lower_case = message.lower()
print(lower_case) # Output: hello, world!


message = "Hello, World!"
upper_case = message.upper()
print(upper_case) # Output: HELLO, WORLD!
```

3.2 Replacing Characters:

- The `replace()` function allows us to replace specific characters or substrings within a string.

- Example:

```
message = "Hello, World!"
new_message = message.replace("World", "Python")
print(new_message) # Output: Hello, Python!
```

3.3 Splitting Strings:

- The `split()` function splits a string into a list of substrings based on a specified delimiter.

- Example: `message = "Hello, Python!"`, `split_message = message.split(" ")` -> `split_message` would be ["Hello,", "Python!"].

Conclusion:

Mastering string manipulation is crucial for any Python programmer, as strings are commonly encountered in various projects. We explored important concepts such as indexing, concatenation, string slicing, modifying case, replacing characters, and splitting strings. Equipped with this knowledge and armed with practical examples and illustrations, you are now ready to wield the power of string manipulation to build robust Python applications.

Working With Lists, Tuples, And Dictionaries:

In this section, we will explore the fundamentals of working with lists, tuples, and dictionaries in Python. These data structures are essential in programming as they allow us to store and manipulate collections of values efficiently. We will dive into each data structure separately, understanding their features, functions, and how they can be utilized in various scenarios. With the help of illustrations and examples, we aim to provide a comprehensive understanding of these powerful data structures.

1. Lists:

Lists are one of the most commonly used data structures in Python. They are mutable, ordered, and allow duplicate values. A list can store a collection of different data types such as integers, strings, or even other lists. To create a list, we use square brackets ([]). For instance:

```
```

```
my_list = [1, 2, 3, 'Python', True]
```

- Indexing and Slicing: Lists can be accessed using indexing, where each element is assigned an index number. The first element has an index of 0, the second has an index of 1, and so on. We can also use slicing to extract a portion of a list based on a range of indices.

```
my_list[0]  # Output: 1
my_list[1:4]  # Output: [2, 3, 'Python']
```

- Mutability: Lists are mutable, meaning their elements can be modified after they are created. We can change, add, or remove elements from a list.

```
my_list[3] = 'Java'  # Modify an element
print(my_list) # Output: [1, 2, 3, 'Java', True]

my_list.append('C++')  # Add an element at the end of the list
print(my_list) # Output: [1, 2, 3, 'Python', True, 'C++']

del my_list[2]  # Remove an element by index
print(my_list) # Output: [1, 2, 'Python', True]
```

2. **Tuples**:

Tuples are similar to lists but are immutable, meaning their elements cannot be modified after creation. Tuples are typically used to store related pieces of information. They are created using parentheses (()).

```
my_tuple = (1, 2, 3, 'Python')
```

- Accessing Elements: We can access tuple elements using indexing, similar to lists.

```
my_tuple[2]  # Output: 3
```

- Immutability: Tuples cannot be modified. Once created, their elements remain constant.

```
my_tuple[2] = 5  # This will raise an error
```

3. Dictionaries:

Dictionaries are an unordered collection of key-value pairs. They are mutable and allow efficient retrieval of values using their associated keys.

To define a dictionary, we use curly braces ({}) and separate each key-value pair with a colon (:).

```
my_dict = {'name': 'John', 'age':25, 'country': 'USA'}
```

- Accessing Values: We can retrieve values from a dictionary by using their corresponding keys.

```
my_dict['age']  # Output: 25
```

- Adding, Modifying, and Removing Elements: We can add new key-value pairs, modify existing ones, or remove entries from a dictionary.

```
my_dict['occupation'] = 'Engineer'  # Add a new key-value pair

my_dict['age'] = 26  # Modify an existing value

del my_dict['country']  # Remove a key-value pair
```

Illustrative Examples:

- Example 1: Finding The Average Of A List Of Numbers:

Suppose we have a list of numbers, and we need to find their average. We can achieve this by summing all the numbers in the list and then dividing the sum by the total number of elements in the list.

```
numbers = [4, 6, 8, 10, 12]

sum_of_numbers = sum(numbers)

average = sum_of_numbers / len(numbers)

print(average)  # Output: 8.0
```

- Example 2: Creating A Student Dictionary With Multiple Attributes:

Let's say we want to store information about a student, such as their name, grade, and subjects. We can use a dictionary to represent this information.

```
student = {'name': 'Alice', 'grade': 9, 'subjects': ['Math', 'Science', 'English']}

print(student['name'])  # Output: Alice

print(student['subjects'][1])  # Output: Science
```

These examples illustrate how lists, tuples, and dictionaries are used to solve real-world problems and represent complex data structures efficiently.

In conclusion, mastering the concepts of lists, tuples, and dictionaries in Python is crucial for effectively managing and manipulating data in various programming scenarios. Through this section, we have covered their features, functions, and provided illustrative examples to solidify your understanding.

Understanding Functions And Their Usage:

In this section, we will explore the concept of functions in Python programming language. Functions are blocks of organized and reusable code that perform specific tasks. They allow us to break down complex programming problems into smaller, more manageable parts.

1. Introduction To Functions:

- A function is defined using the `def` keyword, followed by the function name and parentheses.

- Functions may take input parameters, which are enclosed within the parentheses.

- The code block inside a function is indented and executed when the function is called.

Example:

```python
def greet():
    print("Hello, welcome to Python programming!")
```

greet() # Calling the function
```

Output:

```
Hello, welcome to Python programming!
```

2. Function Parameters And Arguments:

- Parameters are variables that hold the arguments passed to a function.

- Arguments are the values passed into a function when it is called.

Example:

```python

def greet(name):

    print("Hello,", name, "welcome to Python programming!")


greet("John")
```

Output:

```
Hello, John, welcome to Python programming!

```

3. Return Statement:

- Functions can return values using the `return` statement.

- Returned values can be assigned to variables or used in expressions.

Example:

```python
def add_numbers(a, b):
    return a + b
result = add_numbers(5, 3)
print("The sum is:", result)
```

Output:

```
The sum is: 8
```

4. Built-In Functions:

- Python provides many built-in functions that perform commonly used tasks.

- Built-in functions can be called directly without explicitly defining them.
```

Example:

```python
print("Hello, Python!")
length = len("Python")
max_value = max(4, 8, 2)
```

Output:

```
Hello, Python!
6
8
```

5. User-defined Functions:

- Apart from built-in functions, we can create our own custom functions.

- User-defined functions improve code reusability and readability.

Example:

```python
def calculate_area(length, width):
    return length * width
```

```
room_area = calculate_area(10, 5)

print("The area of the room is:", room_area)
```

Output:

```
The area of the room is: 50
```

These are the essential concepts related to functions in Python programming. By understanding functions and their usage, you can write more efficient and modular code to solve complex problems. So, make sure to practice and experiment with functions to gain proficiency in Python programming.

Scope And Parameter Passing In Functions:
Introduction:

In Python, functions are an essential part of the programming language. Understanding the concepts of scope and parameter passing in functions is crucial to becoming a proficient Python programmer. This section will cover these concepts in detail, providing explanations, illustrations, and examples to facilitate a comprehensive understanding.

1. Scope In Functions:

When discussing scope, we refer to the visibility and accessibility of variables in different parts of a program. In Python, variables can have different scopes, which determine where they can be used.

a) Local Scope:

Local scope refers to variables that are defined within a specific function and are only accessible within that function. These variables cannot be accessed from outside the function. Once the function execution is complete, the local variables are destroyed.

b) Global Scope:

Global scope refers to variables that are defined outside of any function and can be accessed from anywhere within the program. These variables have a broader scope and longer lifespan compared to local variables.

Illustration:

```python
def my_function():
    local_variable = 10
    print(local_variable)  # Prints 10

my_function()
print(local_variable)  # Throws an error: NameError: name 'local_variable' is not defined
```

Explanation:

In the above example, the variable `local_variable` is defined within the scope of the function `my_function()`. It is accessible and can be printed within the function, but if we try to access it outside the function, it results in a `NameError`.

2. Parameter Passing In Functions:

When calling a function, we can pass values to it through parameters. Parameters act as placeholders for the values that will be passed to the function during its execution.

a) Positional Parameters:

Positional parameters are defined in a function's parentheses and receive arguments in the same order. The number of arguments passed must match the number of parameters defined.

Example:

```python
def add_numbers(num1, num2):
    return num1 + num2

result = add_numbers(5, 3)  # Passing 5 and 3 as arguments
print(result)  # Prints 8
```

Explanation:

In the above example, the `add_numbers()` function takes two positional parameters `num1` and `num2`. When calling the function and passing `5` and `3` as arguments, the function performs the addition and returns the result, which is then printed.

b) Keyword Arguments:

Keyword arguments are passed to a function by explicitly mentioning the parameter name and its corresponding value. This allows flexibility in reordering or skipping parameters while calling a function.

Example:

```python
def greet_person(name, age):
    print(f"Hello {name}, you are {age} years old!")

greet_person(age=25, name="Alice")  # Passing arguments using keywords
```

Explanation:

In the above example, the `greet_person()` function takes two keyword parameters `name` and `age`. By using keywords to pass arguments, we can specify the order of arguments differently while calling the function. The output will be "Hello Alice, you are 25 years old!"

Conclusion:

Understanding scope and parameter passing in functions is vital for effective Python programming. By mastering these concepts, beginners can write more efficient and flexible code. Use the provided explanations, illustrations, and examples as a reference to strengthen your understanding and proficiency in Python.

Recursion And Its application

In Python programming, recursion refers to the ability of a function to call itself from within its body. This powerful concept allows us to solve complex problems by breaking them down into smaller, more manageable subproblems.

Understanding The Basics Of Recursion:

Recursion relies on two key elements:

1. Base case: This is the simplest possible case that can be solved directly without any further recursion. It acts as a termination condition for the recursive calls and prevents infinite loops.

2. Recursive case: This is the part of the function where the problem is broken down into smaller subproblems, and the function calls itself to solve those subproblems.

Recursive functions have the following general structure:

```
def recursive_function(parameters):
    if base_case:
        return base_case_solution
    else:
        # Recursive case
```

```
return recursive_function(modified_parameters)
```

Illustration With Factorial Function:

Let's understand recursion with a commonly used example - the factorial function. The factorial of a non-negative integer n, denoted as n!, is the product of all positive integers less than or equal to n.

```
def factorial(n):
    if n == 0:
        return 1
    else:
        return n * factorial(n-1)
```

Explanation:

- In the above recursive function, the base case is when n equals 0, where we know that 0! is 1.

- In the recursive case, the function calls itself with the modified parameter of n-1.

- Each recursive call gets closer to the base case until the condition n == 0 is met, and the function starts returning the cumulative product of `n` and each recursive call.

Example:

```
print(factorial(5))
```

Output:

```
120
```

Recursion And Its Application:

Recursion is incredibly useful when dealing with tasks that naturally exhibit a recursive structure or repetitive subproblems. Here are some common applications:

1. Mathematical Computation:

- Factorial calculation, as described above.

- Fibonacci sequence: Each number is the sum of the two preceding ones.

- Exponentiation: Computing powers of a number using repeated multiplications.

2. Tree And Graph Structures:

- Traversing and searching in binary trees, such as Preorder, Inorder, and Postorder traversal.

- Depth-First Search (DFS) and Breadth-First Search (BFS) in graph traversal.

3. Divide and Conquer Algorithms:

- QuickSort and MergeSort: Sorting algorithms that recursively divide the input into smaller sub-arrays.

- Binary Search: Searching in a sorted array by dividing it into halves.

4. Dynamic Programming:

- Optimal substructure problems like the Knapsack problem, Fibonacci series with memoization.

Remembered Tips:

- Always ensure your recursive function has a well-defined base case to avoid infinite recursion.

- Recursive functions can be memory-intensive due to holding multiple function calls on the stack. This can be mitigated using memoization and tail recursion techniques.

In conclusion, recursion is a powerful technique that allows us to solve complex problems by dividing them into smaller, more manageable subproblems. By understanding the basics of recursion and its various applications, you can enhance your problem-solving skills in the Python programming language.

Chapter End Exercises

Multiple Choice Questions:

1. What is the purpose of zero-based indexing in Python strings?

A) It simplifies string manipulation operations.

B) It aligns with the binary representation of characters.

C) It allows for efficient memory allocation.

D) It facilitates easy extraction and manipulation of individual characters.

2. Which function is used to determine the length of a string in Python?

A) string.length()

B) string.size()

C) len(string)

D) length(string)

3. What does the split() function do in Python?

A) Splits a string into individual characters.

B) Splits a string into substrings based on a specified delimiter.

C) Splits a string into equal-sized chunks.

D) Splits a string into words of equal length.

4. What is the key difference between lists and tuples in Python?

A) Lists are immutable, while tuples are mutable.

B) Lists are ordered and allow duplicate values, while tuples are unordered and do not allow duplicates.

C) Lists are created using parentheses (()), while tuples are created using square brackets ([]).

D) Lists can store multiple data types, while tuples can only store integers.

5. Which of the following is a characteristic of recursion in Python?

A) Recursion can only be used with mathematical computations.

B) Recursion relies on two key elements: the base case and the recursive case.

C) Recursion always leads to better performance compared to iterative solutions.

D) Recursion is primarily used for traversing binary trees and graphs.

True/False Statements:

Python strings are immutable, meaning their contents cannot be changed after they are created.
- True
- False

Tuples in Python are mutable data structures.
- True
- False

The split () function in Python splits a string into individual characters.
- True
- False

Recursion is a technique that involves a function calling itself directly or indirectly in its own definition.
- True
- False

Functions in Python cannot return any values.
- True
- False

Coding Practice

1. Write a Python function that takes a string as input and returns the string in reverse order. For example, if the input is "hello", the output should be "olleh".
2. Write a Python function that takes a list of numbers as input and returns the sum of all the numbers in the list.
3. Write a Python function that takes a tuple of integers as input and returns the product of all the integers in the tuple.
4. Write a Python function that takes a dictionary as input and returns a list of keys sorted in alphabetical order.
5. Write a recursive Python function to compute the Fibonacci sequence up to a specified number of terms. The Fibonacci sequence is characterized by the fact that every number after the first two is the sum of the two preceding ones. For example, the Fibonacci sequence up to 5 terms is [0, 1, 1, 2, 3].

Chapter 5: File Handling and Error Handling

A. Reading And Writing Files In Python:

Introduction:

In Python, reading and writing files is an essential skill to master as it allows you to work with data and information stored in various file formats. This section focuses on providing readers, especially beginners, with a comprehensive understanding of file input and output operations in Python. From opening and closing files to performing various read and write operations, this chapter will equip you with the necessary knowledge and examples to manipulate files effectively.

1. Opening And Closing Files:

It is crucial to open a file before performing any operations on it. Python provides a built-in function, `open(),` to open files. This function requires the file name along with the mode in which you want to open the file, such as 'r' for reading, 'w' for writing, or 'a' for appending. It's equally essential to remember to close the file after usage to free up system resources and avoid any potential data loss.

```Python

file = open("file.txt", "r") # Opening file.txt in read mode

# File operations...

file.close() # Closing the file

```

2. Reading Files:

Reading files enables you to extract data and use it within your Python program. Python provides various methods to read file contents, including reading the entire file at once or reading it line by line. The most common methods are:

a. Read The Entire File:

The `read()` function allows you to read the entire contents of a file.

```python
file = open("file.txt," "r")
content = file.read()
print(content)
file.close()
```

b. Read Lines Of A File:

The `readline()` function enables reading a file line by line, where each call to this function returns the next line.

```python
file = open("file.txt," "r")
line = file.readline()
while line:
    print(line)
```

```
line = file.readline()
file.close()
```

3. Writing To Files:

Writing to files in Python allows you to store processed data or create entirely new files. You can use the `write()` or `writelines()` functions to achieve this.

a. Writing A Single Line:

The `write()` function writes a single line to the file.

```python
file = open("file.txt," "w")
file.write("Hello, World!")
file.close()
```

b. Writing multiple lines:

The `writelines()` function writes multiple lines to the file.

```Python
lines = ["Line 1
", "Line 2
", "Line 3
"]
```

```
file = open("file.txt", "w")

file.writelines(lines)

file.close()
```

4. Appending To Files:

Python also allows appending data to existing files using the 'a' mode while opening the file. It ensures the new content will be added at the end of the file without overwriting existing data.

```python
file = open("file.txt," "a")

file.write("Additional content")

file.close()
```

Conclusion:

Manipulating files in Python is an essential skill to work with real-world data and information. By mastering the concepts of reading and writing files, you can create, modify, and analyze data stored in various file formats. This section provided an in-depth understanding of file operations, including opening and closing files, reading their contents, and performing write and append operations. Remember to practice the concepts discussed here to solidify your understanding and enhance your Python programming abilities.

B. Exception Handling And Error Types:
Introduction:

In any programming language, errors are common and occur frequently. Various factors, such as incorrect syntax, invalid data input, or unexpected behavior, can cause these errors. Python provides a powerful mechanism called "exception handling" to deal with such errors gracefully. This section will introduce you to the concept of exception handling and provide an in-depth understanding of the different error types commonly encountered in Python programming.

1. What Is Exception Handling?

Exception handling is a programming technique that allows us to handle errors or exceptional situations gracefully. Instead of abruptly terminating the program, we can catch and handle these errors in a controlled manner. Python provides a structured way to manage exceptions using the try-except statement.

2. The Try-except Statement:

The try-except statement in Python is used to catch and handle exceptions. The try block contains the code that might raise an exception, while the except block handles the exception if it occurs. The general syntax of a try-except statement is as follows:

```
try:
    # code that might raise an exception

except ExceptionType:
```

    # code to handle the exception

    ```

**3. Handling Specific Exceptions:**

Python offers multiple predefined exception types to handle specific situations. Some common exception types include:

- `ZeroDivisionError`: Raised when dividing a number by zero.

- `TypeError`: Raised when operating on incompatible data types.

- `ValueError`: Raised when a function receives an argument of the correct data type but an invalid value.

- `IndexError`: Raised when trying to access an index outside the range of a list or another iterable.

- `FileNotFoundError`: Raised when attempting to open a file that does not exist.

By specifying the specific exception type in the except clause, we can handle different exceptions differently. Here's an example:

```Python

try:

    x = 10 / 0

except ZeroDivisionError:

    print("Error: Division by zero is not allowed.")

```

4. The else Statement:

Sometimes, we want to execute a piece of code if no exception occurs in the try block. We can use the else statement for this purpose. The code inside the else block executes only if no exception was raised. Here's an example:

```Python

try:

   x = 10 / 2

except ZeroDivisionError:

   print("Error: Division by zero is not allowed.")

else:

   print("The division was successful. Result =", x)

```

5. The Finally Block:

The final block is a section of code that is always executed, regardless of whether an exception occurred or not. It is useful for performing cleanup actions, such as closing files or releasing resources, which must be done regardless of exceptions. Here's an example:

```Python

try:

```
file = open("example.txt," "r")

perform operations on the file

finally:

    file.close() # Always close the file, even if an exception occurred earlier.
```

6. Raising Exceptions:

In addition to handling built-in exceptions, programmers can also raise their exceptions using the `raise` statement. This is useful when we want to indicate an exceptional condition within our code. Here's an example:

```Python
def calculate_square_root(number):
    if number < 0:
        raise ValueError("Cannot calculate square root of a negative number.")
    else:
        return math.sqrt(number)
```

Conclusion:

Exception handling plays a crucial role in writing robust and reliable Python programs. By using the try-except statement, we can catch and handle various types of exceptions, ensuring our code doesn't crash unexpectedly. This section has provided a detailed overview of exception handling and various error types. By familiarizing yourself with these concepts and practicing with illustrative examples, you will be well-equipped to handle exceptions effectively in Python programming.

C. Utilizing Try-Except Blocks:
Introduction:

In Python programming, error handling plays a crucial role in writing robust and reliable code. One of the key approaches to handling errors is by utilizing try-except blocks. This section will guide you through the concepts of try-except blocks, explaining their importance and providing illustrative examples.

1. Understanding Try-Except Blocks:

- The try-except blocks allow you to handle exceptions that occur during the execution of your program.

Enclosing potentially error-prone code within a try block allows you to gracefully catch and handle any exceptions that may arise.

- When an exception occurs inside the try block, the code execution jumps to the corresponding except block to handle the exception.

2. Syntax And Usage:

- The basic syntax of a try-except block is as follows:

```Python
try:
```

```
# Code that may raise an exception

except ExceptionType:

# Code to handle the exception
```

- In this syntax, `ExceptionType` can be a specific exception class or a built-in Python exception like `ValueError` or `TypeError.`

- Multiple except blocks can be used to handle different types of exceptions.

- It is also possible to catch multiple exceptions at once using a common base exception class.

3. Handling Specific Exceptions:

- Specific exceptions can be caught and handled individually using separate except blocks.

- Let's consider an example where we try to divide two numbers:

```Python
try:

    num1 = float(input("Enter the numerator: "))

    num2 = float(input("Enter the denominator: "))

    result = num1 / num2

    print(f"Result: {result}")

except ZeroDivisionError:
```

        print("Error: Division by zero is not allowed!")

    except ValueError:

        print("Error: Please enter valid numeric inputs!")
    ```

   - In this example, if the user enters a non-numeric value or tries to divide by zero, the corresponding except block will execute, providing a relevant error message.

   **4. Handling Multiple Exceptions:**

   - You can handle multiple exceptions using a single except block by specifying multiple exception types within parentheses.

   - Here's an example that handles both `ValueError` and `TypeError`:

    ```Python
    try:
        age = int(input("Enter your age: "))
        if age < 0:
            raise ValueError("Age cannot be negative.")
    except (ValueError, TypeError):
        print("Error: Please enter a valid integer for age!")
    ```
    ```

- In this example, if the user enters a non-integer value or a negative integer for age, the except block will handle it accordingly.

5. Utilizing The Else Block:

- An optional `else` block can be included after all the except blocks.

- The code inside the else block executes only if no exceptions are raised in the try block.

```Python
try:
    file = open("data.txt," "r")
    content = file.read()
    print(content)
except FileNotFoundError:
    print("Error: The file does not exist!")
else:
    file.close()
```

In this example, if a file named "data.txt" does not exist, the except block executes. Otherwise, the file's content is printed, and the file is closed inside the else block.

Conclusion:

Understanding and effectively utilizing try-except blocks is essential for handling exceptions and improving the quality of your Python programs. By following the examples and concepts presented in this section, you can confidently handle potential errors and create more robust and reliable code.

D. Implementing Error Handling In File Operations:

Section: Implementing Error Handling In File Operations:

Introduction:

Error handling is an essential aspect of programming in any language, including Python. In this section, we will explore how to implement error handling in file operations using Python. Error handling enables us to handle unexpected or exceptional situations that may occur during file operations. By implementing error-handling techniques, we can create robust and foolproof programs that gracefully handle errors and provide informative feedback to users.

1. The Try-Except Block:

The try-except block is the fundamental error-handling construct in Python. It allows us to catch and handle exceptions that may occur during file operations. The syntax of a try-except block is as follows:

```
```

try:

Code that may raise an exception

except ExceptionType:

Code to handle the exception
```

## 2. Handling File Not Found Errors:

One common error that can occur when performing file operations is a "FileNotFoundError." This error occurs when the specified file cannot be found or accessed. To handle such errors, we can use a try-except block and catch the "FileNotFoundError" exception. Here's an example:

```Python
try:
    file = open("myfile.txt," "r")
    # Code to perform operations on the file
    file.close() # Close the file after operations are complete
except FileNotFoundError:
    print("File not found or cannot be accessed.")
```

3. Handling Permission Errors:

Another common error that can occur during file operations is a "PermissionError." This error occurs when the user does not have the necessary permissions to perform the requested file operation. To handle such errors, we can catch the "PermissionError" exception. Consider the following example:

```Python
```
```

```
try:
    file = open("myfile.txt," "w")
    # Code to write data to the file
    file.close() # Close the file after writing
except PermissionError:
    print("Permission denied. You do not have write access to the file.")
```

4. Using The "Finally" Keyword:

The "finally" keyword is used in conjunction with the try-except block to specify code that should always be executed, regardless of whether an exception occurs or not. It is commonly used to clean up resources or perform any necessary actions before exiting the block. Here's an example:

```Python
try:
    file = open("myfile.txt," "r")
    # Code to read data from the file
except FileNotFoundError:
    print("File not found or cannot be accessed.")
finally:
    file.close() # Ensure the file is always closed
```

```

### 5. Raising Custom Exceptions:

In addition to handling built-in exceptions, we can also raise our custom exceptions to provide more specific error messages or to handle unique situations in our programs. To raise a custom exception, we can use the "raise" keyword. Here's an example:

```Python
try:
    file = open("myfile.txt," "r")

    if file.size > 1000: # Size limit exceeded
        raise CustomException("File size limit exceeded.")
    # Code to read data from the file
except FileNotFoundError:
    print("File not found or cannot be accessed.")
except for CustomException as e:
    print(str(e))
finally:
    file.close()
```

Conclusion:
```

Implementing error handling in file operations is crucial for creating robust and reliable programs. By utilizing the try-except block, we can gracefully handle exceptions such as FileNotFoundErrors and PermissionErrors. Additionally, the finally keyword allows us to perform necessary cleanup actions and raise custom exceptions to handle unique situations. By applying these error-handling techniques, we enhance the user experience and create more resilient Python programs.

Chapter End Exercises

Multiple Choice Questions:

1. What is the primary purpose of implementing error handling in file operations?

a) To increase the speed of file operations

b) To gracefully handle unexpected or exceptional situations

c) To minimize the size of the code

d) To prevent file corruption

2. Which keyword specifies code that should always be executed, regardless of whether an exception occurs?

a) try

b) except

c) finally

d) raise

3. Which error occurs when the specified file cannot be found or accessed?

a) FileNotFoundError

b) PermissionError

c) IOError

d) ValueError

4. In Python, how can custom exceptions be raised?

a) Using the try-except block

b) Using the raise keyword

c) Using the final block

d) Using the if-else statement

5. Which of the following statements is true about the try-except block?

a) It executes the code only if no exceptions occur

b) It executes the code and raises exceptions afterward

c) It allows us to catch and handle exceptions

d) It is not recommended to use in Python programming

True/False Statements:
1. The try-except block allows us to handle exceptions gracefully by catching them and providing alternative paths for execution.
    - True
    - False

2. The final keyword specifies code that should always be executed, regardless of whether an exception occurs.
    - True
    - False

3. FileNotFoundError occurs when a specified file cannot be found or accessed during file operations in Python.
    - True
    - False

4. Custom exceptions can only be raised using the try-except block and not directly within the code.
    - True
    - False

5. The try-except block executes the code only if no exceptions occur, and if an exception occurs, it is raised afterward.
    - True
    - False

Coding Practice
1. **File Backup Script:**
   Write a Python script that takes the name of a file as input from the user and creates a backup of that file by appending the current date and time to the filename. Ensure that the script handles FileNotFoundError gracefully by informing the user if the specified file does not exist.
2. **Word Counter:**
   Create a Python program that reads the contents of a text file and counts the frequency of each word in the file. Store the word frequencies in a dictionary and then write the results to a new text file. Ensure that your program handles FileNotFoundError and IOError appropriately.
3. **CSV Data Validation:**
   Write a Python script that reads data from a CSV file and performs validation checks on the data. For example, you could check if certain columns contain only numeric values or if certain fields meet specific criteria. Implement error handling to handle exceptions like ValueError for data conversion errors.
4. **Log File Analyzer:**
   Develop a Python program that analyzes a log file generated by a web server. The program should extract relevant information such as the number of requests, unique IP addresses, and HTTP status codes. Ensure your program gracefully handles exceptions like FileNotFoundError and properly closes the file after reading.
5. **Temperature Converter with Error Handling:**
   Create a Python script that prompts the user to input a temperature in Celsius and then converts it to Fahrenheit. Implement error handling to handle ValueError in case the user enters a non-numeric value. Additionally, handle the possibility of a

ZeroDivisionError if the conversion formula encounters an issue.

Chapter 6: Object-Oriented Programming With Python

A. Introduction To Object-Oriented Programming (OOP):

In this section, we will explore the major concept of object-oriented programming (OOP). OOP is a powerful programming model that allows us to organize our code into objects, making it more modular, reusable, and maintainable. In this section, we will explore the basics of OOP using the Python programming language, along with illustrations and examples to help strengthen our thinking.

1. **Understanding Objects:**

Object-oriented programming revolves around the concept of objects. An object is an example of a class representing an exact entity or concept in our program. For example, an object of the "Car" class can represent a specific car with unique features and behaviors.

To illustrate this, let's consider a simple example. Imagine we want to model a car in our program. We can define a class called "car" that would have characteristics like color, model, and fuel, and methods like "drive" and "refuel." By creating objects of the "Car" class, we can represent different cars in our program.

2. **Class And Object Relationship:**

A class serves as a blueprint or template for creating objects. It defines the traits and behaviors that an object of that class should have. Consider a class as a cookie cutter and objects as the cookies that are created using that cookie cutter.

In Python, we define a class using the "class" keyword. Let's take a look at an example:

```Python
class Car:
    def __init__(self, color, model):
        self.color = color
        self.model = model

    def drive(self):
        print (f"The {self.color} {self.model} is driving.")

    def refuel(self):
        print (f"The {self.color} {self.model} is refueling.")
```

In the above example, we defined a "Car" class with attributes like color and model and methods like drive and refuel.

3. **Creating Objects:**

Once we have defined a class, we can create many objects of that class. Each object will have its own unique set of attributes and can invoke the defined methods.

```python
```

```
my_car = Car("Red," "Sedan")

your_car = Car("Blue", "SUV")
```

In the above sample, we created two objects, "my_car" and "your_car," by calling the "Car" class and passing the necessary arguments.

4. **Accessing Attributes And Invoking Methods:**

To access the attributes of an object, we use the dot notation. For instance, to access the color attribute of "my_car," we can use "my_car.color."

```Python
print(my_car.color) # Output: Red

my_car.drive() # Output: The red sedan is driving.
```

In the above example, we accessed the color attribute of "my_car" and invoked the drive method.

5. **Encapsulation, Inheritance, And Polymorphism:**

Object-oriented programming also introduces the concepts of encapsulation, inheritance, and polymorphism, which are beyond the scope of this section. However, they form the pillars of OOP and provide additional benefits in organizing and structuring our code.

Encapsulation allows us to bind data and methods together within a class, hiding the internal implementation from the outside world.

Inheritance enables us to create new classes based on existing ones, inheriting their attributes and behaviors. This promotes code reuse and enhances code organization.

Polymorphism allows objects of different classes to be used interchangeably, providing flexibility and modularity in our code.

Conclusion:

In this section, we introduce the concept of object-oriented programming (OOP) in Python. We covered the basics, including the definition of objects and classes, creating objects, accessing attributes, and invoking methods. Additionally, we touched upon other essential OOP concepts like encapsulation, inheritance, and polymorphism. By implementing OOP principles, you'll be able to write more modular, reusable, and maintainable code.

B. Classes And Objects In Python
Introduction:

In Python, classes and objects form the backbone of object-oriented programming (OOP). Understanding these concepts is crucial for beginners to develop scalable and efficient applications. This section will guide you through the fundamentals of classes and objects in Python, providing detailed explanations along with illustrations and examples.

1. **What are classes?**

A class is a blueprint or template that defines the properties and behaviors of an object. It acts as a user-defined data type, encapsulating attributes (variables) and methods (functions) within a single entity. Classes provide a way to organize and structure code, making it more manageable and reusable.

Illustration:

Imagine a class "Car." It can have attributes like color, model, and brand, as well as methods like acceleration and brake.

Example Code:

```
class Car:
    def __init__(self, color, model, brand):
        self.color = color
        self.model = model
        self.brand = brand
    def accelerate(self):
        print (The Car is accelerating.")
    def brake(self):
        print (The Car is braking.")
```

2. **What are objects?**

An object is an instance of a class. It represents a specific entity that can access the attributes and methods defined in its corresponding class. Multiple objects can be created from a single class, each having its unique state and behavior.

Illustration:

Instances of the "Car" class, such as "my_car" or "friend_car," are objects with their specific color, model, and brand attributes.

Example Code:

```
my_car = Car ("Red," "Sedan," "Toyota")

friend_car = Car ("Blue," "SUV," "Ford")

my_car.accelerate() # Output: The Car is accelerating.

print(friend_car.brand) # Output: Ford
```

3. **Class Constructors:**

Constructors are special methods within a class used for initializing object attributes. In Python, the constructor method is called `__init__(),` which gets automatically executed when a new object is created. It allows us to set initial values for object attributes.

Illustration:

When a new car object is created, the `__init__()` method in the "Car" class initializes the object attributes color, model, and brand.

Example Code:

```
def __init__(self, color, model, brand):

    self.color = color

    self.model = model

    self.brand = brand
```

4. **Class Methods:**

Methods are functions defined within a class that perform specific actions on its objects. These methods operate on object attributes and can modify or retrieve their values. They are accessed using dot notation.

Illustration:

The "accelerate()" and "brake()" methods in the "Car" class define a car object's behavior when it accelerates or brakes.

Example :

```
def accelerate(self):

    The Car is accelerating."

def brake(self):

    The Car is braking."
```

5. Accessing Object Attributes And Methods:

To access an object's attributes and methods, we use the dot notation (object.attribute/object.method()). This notation allows us to retrieve or modify the values associated with an object.

Illustration:

The code snippet demonstrates how to access the brand attribute of an object and invoke a method.

Example Code:

```
```

print (friend_car.brand) # Output: Ford

my_car.accelerate() # Output: The Car is accelerating.

```
```

Conclusion:

Understanding classes and objects is essential for creating modular and reusable code in Python. By defining classes, you can group related attributes and behaviors, allowing for efficient organization and extension of your programs. Objects provide individual instances of these classes, enabling you to work with specific data and perform actions on them. With the help of the provided illustrations and examples, you can now confidently start applying classes and objects in Python programming.

C. Inheritance, Polymorphism, And Encapsulation:

Introduction:

In the world of object-oriented programming, Python offers powerful tools to create robust and modular code. Inheritance, polymorphism, and encapsulation are fundamental concepts in Python that allow programmers to write efficient and maintainable code. This section will delve into these concepts, providing clear explanations, illustrations, and practical examples.

Inheritance:

Inheritance is the ability to create new classes from existing classes. It allows the derived class (also known as a subclass) to inherit attributes and methods from the base class (also known as the superclass). This promotes code reuse and enables the creation of specialized classes.

Illustration:

Consider a base class called `Vehicle` that has attributes such as `color` and methods like 'start_engine().` Now, we can create a derived class called `Car` that inherits the attributes and methods from `Vehicle` and has additional attributes and methods specific to cars, like `accelerate().`

Example:

```Python

class Vehicle:

    def __init__(self, color):
```

```
        self.color = color

    def start_engine(self):

        print("Engine started!")

class Car(Vehicle):

    def __init__(self, color, model):

        super().__init__(color)

        self.model = model

    def accelerate(self):

        print("Car accelerated!")

Creating an instance of Car

my_car = Car ("Blue", "Sedan")

print(my_car.color) # Output: Blue

my_car.start_engine() # Output: Engine started!

my_car.accelerate() # Output: Car accelerated!
```

Polymorphism:

Polymorphism allows objects of different classes to be treated as objects of a common class. This means that a single function can work with objects of multiple classes as long as they implement the same methods. It promotes flexibility and extensibility in code.

Illustration:

Consider the common method `play_sound()` that can be used for different types of animals. This method can invoke specific sounds depending on the type of object, such as a dog barking or a cat meowing. The method only needs to know that the object has a `play_sound()` method, irrespective of the class.

Example:

```Python
class Dog:

    def play_sound(self):

        print("Bark!")

class Cat:

    def play_sound(self):

        print("Meow!")

# Polymorphic function

def make_sound(animal):

    animal.play_sound()

Creating objects

dog = Dog()

cat = Cat()

Calling the polymorphic function

make_sound(dog) # Output: Bark!
```

make_sound(cat) # Output: Meow!

```

### Encapsulation:

Encapsulation is the practice of hiding a class's internal implementation details and exposing only the necessary interfaces to interact with it. It prevents direct access to sensitive data, thereby improving code maintainability and security.

### Illustration:

Consider a class `BankAccount` where the balance attribute should not be accessible directly. Instead, it should be accessed through methods like `deposit()` and `withdraw(),` which handle the logic and keep the balance in a valid state.

### Example:

```Python

class BankAccount:

    def __init__(self):

        self.__balance = 0# Encapsulated attribute

    def deposit(self, amount):

        self.__balance += amount

    def withdraw(self, amount):

        if self.__balance >= amount:

            self.__balance -= amount

```
        else:
            print("Insufficient balance!")
    # Encapsulated attribute getter method
    def get_balance(self):
        return self.__balance

Creating an instance of BankAccount
account = BankAccount()
account.deposit(100)
account.withdraw(50)
print(account.get_balance()) # Output: 50
```

Conclusion:

Understanding inheritance, polymorphism, and encapsulation in Python is crucial for writing efficient, modular, and maintainable code. In this section, we explored these concepts with clear explanations, illustrations, and practical examples, enabling beginners to grasp these concepts effectively and apply them to their Python programming journey.

D. Working With Modules And Packages:

In Python, modules and packages are essential components that help organize and manage code. Understanding how to work with modules and packages is crucial for creating larger Python projects and collaborating with other developers.

Introduction:

Modules in Python are simply files containing Python code that defines functions, variables, and classes. They enable code reuse and allow code to be separated into logical units. Packages, on the other hand, are directories that contain multiple modules organized in a hierarchical structure.

Importing Modules:

To use code from a module, you need to import it into your current code file. Python provides different ways to import modules based on your needs:

Importing The Entire Module:

```Python

import module_name

```

This imports the entire module and allows you to access its contents using the ```module_name``` prefix.

Importing Specific Items From A Module:

```

Python

from module_name import item_name

```

This imports a specific item (function, variable, or class) from the module and makes it directly accessible without needing to use the module's prefix.

Importing The Entire Module With An Alias:

```Python
import module_name as alias
```

This imports the entire module as an alias, allowing you to access its contents using the alias instead of the full module name.

Importing All Items From A Module:

```Python
from module_name import *
```

This imports all items from the module into the current namespace. However, it is generally discouraged as it can lead to namespace clashes.

Creating Modules:

You can easily create your modules by writing Python code in a separate file with a ```.py``` extension. Let's say we have a file named ```math_operations.py``` containing the following code:

```Python
def add(x, y):
    return x + y
```

```
def subtract(x, y):

    return x - y
```

To use these functions in another Python file, we can import the module as follows:

```
Python

import math_operations

result = math_operations.add(5, 3)

print(result)
```

Output: 8

```
```

Creating Packages:

Packages allow you to organize related modules into a folder hierarchy. To create a package, you need to create a directory with a special file called ```__init__.py``` in it. This file can be empty or contain an initialization code.

Let's assume we have the following package structure:

```
my_package/

__init__.py
```

module1.py

module2.py

```

To use modules from this package, we can import them like this:

```python

import my_package.module1

```

Or, if we prefer shorter syntax:

```Python

from my_package import module2

```

Special Package/Module Import Techniques

Importing Multiple Items From A Module:

```

Python

from module_name import item1, item2, item3

```

This allows importing multiple items from a module in a single line.

Importing All Items From A Module Except One:
```

```Python
from module_name import *
del module_name.unwanted_item
```

This imports all items from a module and then deletes the unwanted item from the namespace.

Conclusion:

Understanding how to work with modules and packages is essential for organizing and managing your Python code effectively. By utilizing modules and packages, you can improve code reusability, readability, and collaboration with other developers. Remember to structure your code into logical units and use proper importing techniques to make your codebase more maintainable.

Illustrations And Examples:

Importing An Entire Module:

```Python
import math
print(math.sqrt(16))
```

Output: 4.0

```

**Importing Specific Items From A Module:**
```

```Python
from random import randint
print(randint(1, 10))
```

Output (a random number between 1 and 10):
```
```

Importing An Entire Module With An Alias:

```Python
import datetime as dt
print(dt.datetime.now())
```

Output:
```
2024-03-09 19:25:55.590410
```

Creating A Package And Using Modules From It:

Assume The Following Package Structure:

```
my_package/
    __init__.py
    module1.py
```

module2.py

```

```python
from my_package import module1, module2
module1.some_function()
module2.some_other_function()
```

Output:

```
This is module 1.
This is module 2.
```

Remember to practice these concepts and experiment with different scenarios to solidify your understanding of working with modules and packages in Python.
```

Chapter End Exercises

Multiple Choice Questions:

1. **What is the primary purpose of object-oriented programming (OOP)?**
   a) To write concise programs

   b) To organize code into objects for better modularity and reusability

   c) To optimize code execution speed

   d) To eliminate the need for functions

2. **Which keyword is used to define a class in Python?**
   a) class

   b) def.

   c) Object

   d) Struct

3. **What is inheritance in object-oriented programming?**
   a) The process of creating objects from classes

   b) The process of creating classes from objects

   c) The ability to create new classes based on existing ones

   d) The ability to create new objects with unique attributes

4. **Which concept allows objects of different classes to be treated as objects of a common class?**
   a) Inheritance

b) Polymorphism

c) Encapsulation

d) Abstraction

5. **What is the purpose of encapsulation in OOP?**
   a) To bind data and methods together within a class

   b) To create new classes from existing ones

   c) To treat objects of different classes interchangeably

   d) To organize related attributes and behaviors together

True and False:

1. **Inheritance allows a class to inherit attributes and methods from multiple other classes.**

    (True/False)

2. **Polymorphism allows objects of different classes to be used interchangeably.**

    (True/False)

3. **Encapsulation hides the internal implementation details of a class and exposes only the necessary interfaces.**

    (True/False)

4. **Modules in Python are directories that contain multiple packages.**

    (True/False)

5. **Using "from module_name import *" is generally encouraged as it simplifies the code.**

    (True/False)

Coding Practice

1. **Class and Object Creation** Create a Python class called **Rectangle** with attributes **length** and **width**. Implement methods to calculate the Rectangle's area and perimeter. Create two instances of the **Rectangle** class and print their area and perimeter.

2. **Inheritance** Create a base class called **Shape** with a method **calculate_area()** and a derived class called **Square** that inherits from **Shape**. Implement the **calculate_area()** method in both classes to calculate the area of a square. Create an instance of the **Square** class and print its area.

3. **Polymorphism** Define two classes: **Circle** and **Triangle**. Both classes should have a method **calculate_area()**. Implement the method differently in each class to calculate the area of a circle and a triangle, respectively. Create instances of both classes and call their **calculate_area()** methods.

4. **Encapsulation** Create a class called **BankAccount** with private attributes **balance** and **account_number**. Implement methods of **deposit()** and **withdraw()** to modify the balance. Ensure that the **balance** attribute cannot be accessed directly from outside the class. Test your class by creating an instance of **BankAccount** and performing deposits and withdrawals.

5. **Modules and Packages** Create a Python module named **math_operations** with functions to add, subtract, multiply, and divide two numbers. Import this module into another Python script and use its functions to perform arithmetic operations.

Chapter 7: Advanced Python Concepts
A. Regular Expressions And Their Usage:

Introduction:

In this section, we will explore the concept of regular expressions and how they can be used in Python programming. Regular expressions, often referred to as regex, are powerful tools that allow us to define specific patterns to match or search for strings in a text. They are extensively used in various applications, such as data validation, search algorithms, and text processing. Understanding and utilizing regular expressions effectively is an essential skill for any Python programmer. In this section, we will cover the basics of regular expressions and provide illustrative examples to help beginners grasp the concept.

1. What Are Regular Expressions?

Regular expressions are sequences of characters that define search patterns. These patterns can be used to match, search, or manipulate text data. A regular expression consists of a combination of regular characters (such as letters, digits, and symbols) and special characters that have specific meanings within the regex syntax. The power of regular expressions lies in their ability to represent complex patterns concisely.

2. The re Module:

Python provides a built-in module called 're' for working with regular expressions. The 're' module offers various functions and methods to work with regular expressions, such as pattern matching, string substitution, and splitting based on patterns. Before using regular expressions, we need to import the 're' module into our Python script.

Illustration:

```Python

import re

```

3. Matching Patterns:

The primary application of regular expressions is to search for specific patterns within strings. We can use regular expression patterns to match a single character, a sequence of characters, or even complex patterns involving repetitions and optional elements.

Illustration:

Matching a Single Character

```Python

import re

pattern = "b[aeiou]t" # Matches "bat," "bet," "bit," "bot," "but."

text = "The bat sat on the mat."

result = re.findall(pattern, text)

print(result)  # Output: ['bat']

```

4. Special Characters And Metacharacters:

Regular expressions utilize special characters, also known as metacharacters, to define patterns more precisely. These metacharacters have special meanings and affect the way patterns are matched. Some commonly used metacharacters include:

- `.` (dot): Matches any single character except a new line.

- `^` (caret): Matches the start of a string or line.

- `$` (dollar): Matches the end of a string or line.

- `*` (asterisk): Matches zero or more occurrences of the preceding element.

- `+` (plus): Matches one or more occurrences of the preceding element.

- `?` (question mark): Matches zero or one occurrence of the preceding element.

- `[]` (square brackets): Defines a character class and matches any single character within the brackets.

Illustration:

Matching Special Characters

```Python
import re

pattern = "The cat .* the .*"

text1 = "The cat sat on the mat."  # Matches pattern

text2 = "The dog jumped over the fence."  # No match

result1 = re.match(pattern, text1)

result2 = re.match(pattern, text2)
```

print(result1) # Output: <re.Match object; span=(0, 23), match='The cat sat on the mat.'>

print(result2) # Output: None

```

### 5. Quantifiers:

Quantifiers offer a way to specify the number of occurrences a pattern should match. They allow us to define patterns that repeat a certain number of times. Some commonly used quantifiers include:

- `*` (asterisk): Matches zero or more occurrences.

- `+` (plus): Matches one or more occurrences.

- `?` (question mark): Matches zero or one occurrence.

- `{m}`: Matches exactly `m` occurrences.

- `{m, n}`: Matches between `m` and `n` occurrences (inclusive).


Illustration: Using Quantifiers

```Python

import re

pattern = "ab{3,5}c" # Matches "abbbc," "abbbbc," "abbbbbc."

text = "The abbbbc pattern is important."

result = re.findall(pattern, text)

print(result)  # Output: ['abbbbc']

```

6. Grouping and Capturing:

Groups in regular expressions allow us to capture and manipulate specific portions of the matched text. We can enclose patterns within parentheses to create groups. These groups can be accessed, referenced later in the regex, or used for extraction and substitution operations.

Illustration:

Grouping and Capturing

```Python

import re

pattern = "(a(b{2,3}c))"

text = "The abbbc pattern is important."

result = re.findall(pattern, text)

print(result)  # Output: [('abbbc', 'bbbc')]

```

Conclusion:

Regular expressions are a powerful tool for searching and manipulating text in Python. This section provides an introduction to regular expressions and their usage. By
```

mastering regular expressions, beginners can significantly enhance their text-processing capabilities within their Python programs. With the knowledge gained from this section, readers can explore more advanced regular expression techniques and apply them to a wide range of practical programming tasks.

B. Multithreading And Multiprocessing:

Introduction:

In Python programming, multithreading and multiprocessing are essential concepts that allow multiple tasks to run concurrently. They help in achieving improved performance and efficiency by utilizing the available system resources effectively. This section will explore the concepts of multithreading and multiprocessing in Python, providing detailed explanations along with relevant illustrations and examples.

1. Multithreading:

1.1 Understanding Threads:

A thread is the smallest unit of execution within a program. Multithreading involves the creation and management of multiple threads that can perform tasks concurrently. Python's `threading` module makes this implementation easy and efficient.

1.2 Benefits of Multithreading:

• Improved responsiveness: Multithreading allows concurrent execution, enabling an application to remain responsive even when performing multiple tasks simultaneously.

- Effective resource utilization: By efficiently utilizing idle CPU cycles, multithreading can optimize system resources, resulting in improved performance.
- Simplified programming model: Python's `threading` module provides a high-level interface, making it easier to implement and manage multiple threads.

1.3 Thread Creation in Python:

To create a thread in Python, follow these steps:

- Import the `threading` module.
- Define a function (task) that the thread will execute.
- Create an instance of the `Thread` class, passing the task function as an argument.
- Call the `start ()` method on the thread instance to initiate execution.

1.4 Example: Multithreading in Python:

Let's understand the concept with an example. Consider a program that needs to perform two independent tasks concurrently: downloading a file and performing a CPU-intensive calculation.

```Python

import threading

def file_download():

    # Download file code here

    pass

def cpu_intensive_calculation():

    # Calculation code here
```

```
    pass

# Create thread instances

download_thread = threading.Thread(target=file_download)

calculation_thread = threading.Thread(target=cpu_intensive_calculation)

# Start the threads

download_thread.start()

calculation_thread.start()
```

2. Multiprocessing:

2.1 Understanding Processes:

Unlike threads, which share the same memory space, processes function as independent entities. Each process has its own memory space, making them more isolated from each other. Python's `multiprocessing` module facilitates the creation and management of multiple processes.

2.2 Benefits of Multiprocessing:

• Enhanced system utilization: By utilizing multiple CPUs or cores, multiprocessing allows for efficient utilization of system resources, resulting in faster execution of tasks.
• Improved stability: Since processes operate independently, errors in one process do not interrupt or affect others, ensuring more robust and stable applications.

- Effective parallelism: Multiprocessing is a powerful approach to achieve parallelism in Python by distributing tasks among multiple processes.

2.3 Process Creation in Python:

- To create a process in Python, follow these steps:
- Import the 'multiprocessing' module.
- Define a function (task) that the process will execute.
- Create an instance of the `Process` class, passing the task function as an argument.
- Call the `start ()` method on the process instance to initiate execution.

2.4 Example: Multiprocessing in Python:

Let's consider an example where a program needs to calculate the square of numbers using two independent processes.

```Python
import multiprocessing

def calculate_square(numbers):

    # Square calculation code here

    pass



# Create process instances

process_1 = multiprocessing.Process(target=calculate_square, args=([1, 2, 3, 4, 5],))
```

```
process_2 = multiprocessing.Process(target=calculate_square, args=([6, 7, 8, 9, 10],))

# Start the processes

process_1.start()

process_2.start()
```
```

## Conclusion:

Multithreading and multiprocessing are essential concepts in Python programming for achieving concurrent execution of tasks. By utilizing the `threading` and `multiprocessing` modules, Python provides robust support for creating and managing multiple threads and processes. This section aims to provide a comprehensive understanding of multithreading and multiprocessing with detailed explanations, illustrations, and examples, enabling beginners to grasp these concepts effectively.

## C. GUI Development With Python Libraries:

### Introduction:

Graphical User Interfaces (GUI) play a crucial role in enhancing the user experience and interactivity within a program or application. In Python, there are several powerful libraries available for GUI development, making it easier for beginners to create visually appealing and user-friendly applications. In this section, we will explore the key Python libraries used for GUI development, along with examples and illustrations.
```

1. Tkinter:

Tkinter is the standard GUI library for Python and supports a wide range of widgets (such as buttons, labels, text boxes, etc.) for creating desktop applications. It provides a simple and intuitive way to build GUIs, making it an ideal choice for beginners. Let's review a simple example that demonstrates a basic Tkinter application:

Example:

```Python
import tkinter as tk

def display_message():
    message = "Hello, GUI World!"
    print(message)

root = tk.Tk()

root.title("My First GUI Application")

button = tk.Button(root, text="Click Me", command=display_message)

button.pack()

root.mainloop()
```

In this example, we import the `tkinter` library and create a function `display_message()` that prints a message. We then create a `Tk` object, set the window title, and create a button widget, which activates the `display_message()` function when clicked. Finally, we use the `mainloop()` method to start the GUI application. This simple program displays a window with a button, which prints the message when clicked.

2. PyQT:

PyQT is another powerful GUI library for Python that provides a comprehensive set of tools for developing cross-platform applications. It is known for its extensive feature set, flexibility, and a large community of contributors. Let's consider an example where we create a basic PyQT application:

Example:

```Python

import sys

from PyQt5.QtWidgets import QApplication, QMainWindow, QLabel, QPushButton


def display_message():

    message = "Hello, PyQT World!"

    print(message)

app = QApplication(sys.argv)

window = QMainWindow()

window.setWindowTitle("My First PyQT Application")

label = QLabel(window)
```

```
label.setText("Welcome to PyQT")

label.move(100, 100)

button = QPushButton(window)

button.setText("Click Me")

button. clicked.connect(display_message)

button.move(100, 200)

window.show()

sys.exit(app.exec_())
```
```

In this example, we import the necessary modules and create a `display_message()` function that prints a message to the console. We then create an `app` object of the `QApplication` class and a `window` object of the `QMainWindow` class. We set the window title, create a label widget, and a button widget that triggers the `display_message()` function when clicked. Finally, we display the window and ensure a clean exit when the application is closed.

### 3. Kivy:

Kivy is an open-source Python library for developing multitouch applications. It has a unique approach to GUI development, focusing on a natural and user-friendly user interface. Kivy supports various input methods such as touch, mouse, pen, and more. Let's explore a simple Kivy application:
```

Example:

```Python
from kivy.app import App
from kivy.uix.label import Label
from kivy.uix.button import Button
class MyApp(App):
    def build(self):
        label = Label(text="Welcome to Kivy")
        def display_message(instance):
            message = "Hello, Kivy World!"
            print(message)
        button = Button(text="Click Me")
        button.bind(on_press=display_message)
        label.add_widget(button)
        return label
MyApp().run()
```

In this example, we import the required modules and create a class `MyApp` that inherits from `App.` Inside the `build()` method, we create a label widget and define the `display_message()` function to print a message. We then create a button widget and bind the `display_message()` function to its `on_press` event. Finally, we add the button to the label widget and return it as the application's root widget.

Conclusion:

In this section, we explored three popular Python libraries for GUI development: Tkinter, PyQT, and Kivy. Each library offers its unique set of features and capabilities. By utilizing their respective tools, beginners can create visually appealing and interactive GUI applications in Python. With the help of code examples and illustrations, you can now dive into GUI development using Python libraries with confidence.

D. Web Scraping And Data Manipulation:

In this section, we will explore the fascinating world of web scraping and data manipulation using Python. Web scraping is the process of extracting data from websites, while data manipulation involves transforming and manipulating the collected data to derive meaningful insights. Python provides numerous powerful libraries and tools that make these tasks easy and efficient.

1. Introduction To Web Scraping:

Web scraping is a technique used to extract data from websites. It allows us to automate the collection of data from multiple web pages without manual intervention. Python offers several libraries, with Beautiful Soup and Selenium being popular choices for web scraping operations. With these libraries, you can extract data from HTML, XML, or other structured formats.

2. Retrieving Website Data With Requests:

The first step in web scraping is sending HTTP requests to websites and receiving their responses. Python's requests library is commonly used for this purpose. We will learn how to send requests, handle responses, and extract required data from the website using the requests library.

Example:

```Python

import requests


response = requests.get('https://example.com')
```

```
print(response.text)
```

This example demonstrates sending a GET request to https://example.com and printing the response's content. It also showcases the basic usage of the Requests library.

3. Parsing HTML With BeautifulSoup:

Once we have retrieved the website content, we need to parse the HTML to extract the desired data. BeautifulSoup is a Python library that makes HTML parsing simple and efficient. It provides tools for traversing, searching, and manipulating the parsed HTML tree structure.

Example:

```Python
from bs4 import BeautifulSoup

html = "<html><body><h1> Hello, Web Scraping!</h1></body></html>"

soup = BeautifulSoup(html, 'html.parser')

print(soup.h1.text) # Output: Hello, Web Scraping!
```

This example shows how to parse an HTML string using BeautifulSoup and extract the text within the `h1` tag. The parsed HTML tree can be easily navigated, and specific elements can be extracted using their tags, classes, or attributes.

4. Automation And Dynamic Website Scraping With Selenium:

Some websites generate content dynamically using JavaScript. To scrape these websites, we need tools that can handle JavaScript and interact with the page elements. Selenium is a powerful Python library that automates browser interactions and enables web scraping of dynamic websites.

Example:

```Python
from selenium import webdriver

driver = webdriver.Chrome()

driver.get('httрs://example.com')

element = driver.find_element_by_tag_name('h1')

print(element.text)
```

This example demonstrates how to use Selenium to automate a browser session, open a webpage, and extract the text of an element. Selenium provides methods to interact with page elements, wait for content to load, click buttons, and much more, enabling powerful web scraping capabilities.

Data Manipulation With Pandas:

Once we have successfully scraped the desired data, we often need to clean, manipulate, and analyze it. The Python library Pandas is widely used for data manipulation and analysis. It provides powerful data structures and functions for data wrangling, filtering, grouping, and much more.

Example:

```Python

import pandas as pd

data = {'Name': ['John', 'Amy', 'Bob'],

'Age': [28, 32, 45],

'City': ['New York', 'London', 'Paris']}

df = pd.DataFrame(data)

print(df.head()) #Output:

```
    Name   Age   City
0   John   28   New York
1   Amy   32   London
2   Bob   45   Paris
```

```

This example showcases how to create a Pandas DataFrame from a dictionary and display its first few rows. Pandas offers various methods for filtering, sorting, aggregating, and transforming data, making it an invaluable tool for data manipulation tasks.

6. Wrapping Up:

Web scraping and data manipulation are essential skills for extracting valuable information from websites and performing data analysis tasks. Python provides a wide range of libraries and tools to make these tasks accessible, even for beginners. With the knowledge gathered from this section, you can dive deeper into the world of web scraping and data manipulation, unlocking endless possibilities for exploring and understanding vast amounts of web data.

Remember always to respect the website's Terms of Use and be mindful of the legal and ethical implications of web scraping.

Chapter End Exercise

Multiple Choice Questions:

1. **What is a regular expression?**
    - A) A sequence of characters used for defining search patterns.
    - B) A Python function for sorting lists.
    - C) A built-in Python module for mathematical operations.
    - D) A method for defining class attributes.
2. **Which module in Python is commonly used for working with regular expressions?**
    - A) os
    - B) math
    - C) re
    - D) sys
3. **What does the re. findall() functions do?**
    - A) It finds all occurrences of a pattern in a string.
    - B) It finds only the first occurrence of a pattern in a string.
    - C) It replaces all occurrences of a pattern with a specified string.
    - D) It compiles a regular expression pattern.
4. **Which metacharacter in regular expressions matches any single character except a newline?**
    - A) ^
    - B) $
    - C) .
    - D) *
5. **What does the {m, n} quantifier specify in regular expressions?**
    - A) Matches exactly m occurrences.
    - B) Matches zero or one occurrence.
    - C) Matches between m and n occurrences.
    - D) Matches one or more occurrences.

True or False:

1) Multithreading allows multiple threads to share the same memory space.

   (True/False)

2) Selenium is a Python library commonly used for parsing HTML.

   (True/False)

3) Pandas is a Python library used for data manipulation and analysis.

   (True/False)

4) requests is a Python library used for sending HTTP requests to websites.

   (True/False)

5) PyQT is a Python library specifically designed for web scraping tasks.

   (True/False)

Coding Practice:

I. Write a Python function that takes a regular expression pattern and a list of strings as input and returns a list of strings that match the pattern.

II. Write a Python program using BeautifulSoup to scrape the titles of all articles from the homepage of a news website (assuming HTML structure with article titles enclosed in <h2> tags).

III. Write a Python function that takes a string of text and returns a dictionary containing the frequency of each word (case-insensitive).

Chapter 8: Debugging And Testing

A. Introduction To Debugging Tools

Introduction:

Debugging is an essential skill for programmers, as it helps identify and fix errors in their code. Python offers various tools and techniques to simplify the debugging process. In this section, we will explore the fundamentals of debugging tools, their importance, and how to incorporate them into your Python coding workflow. We will provide detailed explanations, along with illustrations and examples, to help beginners grasp these concepts effectively.

1. Importance Of Debugging Tools:

Debugging tools are crucial for identifying and resolving bugs in your code. They help you gain a deeper understanding of how your program executes and assist in finding logic errors, syntax mistakes, and runtime issues. By using these tools, you can save significant time and effort in the debugging process.

2. Common Debugging Techniques:

Before diving into specific debugging tools, it's crucial to understand some common techniques used during the debugging process:

a. Print Statements:
Adding print statements at strategic points in your code can help track the flow of execution and pinpoint problem areas. By printing relevant variables or messages, you can identify unexpected behavior or track the value changes during program execution.

b. Error Messages:

Python provides detailed error messages that indicate the location and type of error encountered. Understanding these messages can be immensely helpful in fixing the code.

c. Documentation:
Python's official documentation and external resources offer valuable insights into understanding and resolving common coding issues. Learning how to navigate and utilize these resources effectively can be an advantageous debugging technique.

3. Python Debugging Tools:
a. pdb (Python Debugger):
pdb is a built-in Python library that provides a command-line debugger for interactive debugging. It allows you to step through your code, set breakpoints, examine variables, and trace the program's flow during execution. Through PDB, you can gain precise control over the debugging process and detect the source of bugs effectively.

Example:

```Python
import pdb

def add_numbers(a, b):

    result = a + b

    pdb.set_trace()

    return result

print(add_numbers(5, 3))
```

```

**Output:**

```

> Filename.py(5)add_numbers()

-> return result

(pdb) a

a = 5

b = 3

(pdb) n

> Filename.py(7)add_numbers()

-> return result

(pdb) result

8

(pdb) q

```

In the above example, the pdb.set_trace() function sets a breakpoint during the execution of the add_numbers() function. When executing the program, it pauses at the breakpoint and enters the pdb interactive debugging mode. The "a" command shows the value of variables' a and 'b'; 'n' proceeds to the next line; and 'p' prints the value of the result variable. Finally, 'q' quits the debugger.
```

b. IDE-Specific Debuggers:

Integrated Development Environments (IDEs) like PyCharm, Visual Studio Code, and PyDev provide powerful debugging capabilities tailored for Python. These IDEs offer graphical interfaces, breakpoints, variable inspection, call stack analysis, and other features that make the debugging process more intuitive and efficient. These tools may vary based on the chosen IDE, but the core functionality remains the same.

c. Logging:

Logging is another essential technique for debugging, especially in complex projects. The logging module in Python allows you to generate log messages at various levels, indicating the program's state during execution. By strategically placing logging statements, you can track the flow of your code, capture important variables' values, and track errors or unexpected behavior.

Example:

```Python

import logging

logging.basicConfig(level=logging.DEBUG)

logger = logging.getLogger(__name__)


def divide(a, b):

    logger.debug(f"Dividing {a} by {b}")

    try:

        result = a / b
```

    except ZeroDivisionError:

    logger. error ("Division by zero")

    return None

    return result

result = divide(10, 2)

#Output: DEBUG:__main__:Dividing 10 by 2

```

In this example, logging.basicConfig(level=logging.DEBUG) configures the logger to print all the debug-level messages. By adding a logger.debug() statements, we can track the values of 'a' and 'b' during the division operation. Additionally, logger. error() captures exceptions like the ZeroDivisionError and allows specific error handling.

**Conclusion:**

Understanding the importance of debugging tools and incorporating them into your Python coding workflow is essential for maintaining code quality and efficiency. Whether it's using pdb for interactive debugging, IDE-specific debuggers for a more visually appealing experience, or leveraging the logging module for tracking your code's execution, these tools empower you to identify, analyze, and fix errors efficiently, enhancing your overall programming skills.
```

B. Techniques For Efficient Debugging:

Introduction:

Mastering the art of debugging is a vital skill for any Python programmer, whether you're a beginner or an experienced coder. Debugging allows you to identify and fix errors in your code, increasing the efficiency and reliability of your programs. In this section, we will explore essential techniques, complete with illustrations and examples, to enhance your debugging skills in Python.

Using Print Statements:

One of the simplest yet most effective debugging techniques is using print statements strategically within your code. By inserting print statements at critical sections, you can monitor the values of variables, track program flow, and identify potential issues. Let's consider an example:

```
```
def calculate_average(numbers):

    total = sum(numbers)

    count = len(numbers)

    average = total / count

    print("Total:", total)

    print("Count:", count)

    print("Average:", average)
```
```

```
    return average

numbers = [2, 4, 6, 8]

result = calculate_average(numbers)

#Output:

Total: 20
Count: 4
Average: 5.0
```

By including print statements, we can observe the intermediate values of `total,` `count,` and `average.` This enables us to pinpoint any miscalculations or illogical values.

Utilizing The Debugger:

Python offers a built-in debugger module, `pdb,` that provides further functionality and control during the debugging process. The `pdb` module allows you to set breakpoints, step through your code, and examine variables interactively. Let's illustrate its usage with an example:

```
import pdb

def reverse_string(string):

    reversed_string = ""

    for char in string:
```

```
        pdb.set_trace() # Set breakpoint

        reversed_string = char + reversed_string

        return reversed_string

word = "Python"

reversed_word = reverse_string(word)

```

In this example, we introduce a breakpoint using `pdb.set_trace()` within the 'reverse_string` function. Once the breakpoint is triggered, the debugger will halt execution, allowing you to examine variables' values and step through the code line by line.

Logging:

Another useful debugging technique is logging. Instead of relying on print statements, logging enables you to record events and messages throughout your code, providing a comprehensive picture of the program's execution. This proves especially helpful in larger, more complex projects. An example showcasing logging:

```

import logging

logging.basicConfig(filename='debug.log', level=logging.DEBUG)

def calculate_factorial(n):
```

```
    result = 1

    for i in range (1, n+1):

        logging.debug('i: %s, result: %s' % (i, result))

        result *= i

    return result

factorial = calculate_factorial(5)
```
```

In this example, we configure the logging module to save debug information to a file called `debug.log.` By inserting appropriate logging statements, such as `logging. Debug ()`, we can track the values of variables or relevant details during program execution more precisely.

**Analyzing Stack Traces:**

---

When encountering an error or exception in your code, Python provides a detailed error message called a stack trace. The stack trace provides valuable information, like the line causing the error, the functions involved, and the call sequence. Understanding how to analyze and interpret these stack traces effectively is crucial for debugging. Let's see an example:

```
    ```

    def divide(x, y):
```

```
        result = x / y

        return result

x = 10

y = 0

z = divide(x, y)
```

In this case, when attempting to divide `x` by `y`, a `ZeroDivisionError` will occur. The resulting stack trace pinpoints the line causing the error, allowing you to identify the problem quickly and rectify it.

Conclusion:

Mastering debugging techniques is an essential aspect of becoming a proficient Python programmer. This section covered various techniques, including strategically using print statements, leveraging the built-in debugger module `pdb,` employing logging statements, and analyzing stack traces. By applying these techniques with precision and practice, you will develop a robust skill set to identify and rectify issues swiftly within your Python programs.

C. Writing Test Cases And Performing Unit Testing:

Introduction:

Writing test cases and performing unit testing are essential aspects of software development. Test cases help ensure the correctness, robustness, and reliability of your code, while unit testing allows you to validate individual components or units of your program. In this section, we will explore the concepts, techniques, and best practices for writing test cases and performing unit testing in Python. We will provide clear explanations, accompanied by illustrations and examples, to help you grasp these concepts effectively.

1. Understanding Test Cases:

Test cases are a set of conditions or inputs developed to verify if a code segment or a unit of code behaves as expected. They test various scenarios, including edge cases, to ensure that the program functions correctly in all possible situations. Python provides several frameworks, such as unit test and pytest, that simplify the process of writing and executing test cases.

2. Writing Effective Test Cases:

To write effective test cases, consider the following guidelines:

a) Test cases should be independent and isolated, meaning that the outcome of one test should not affect another.
b) Each test case should have a clear purpose and focus on a specific behavior or functionality.
c) Use meaningful and descriptive names for your test cases, making it easier to identify the failing test case.
d) Cover different scenarios and edge cases to ensure code correctness across various inputs.
e) Test both positive and negative cases, validating the expected as well as unexpected behavior of the code.
f) Avoid hardcoding inputs or expected outputs; instead, use variables or constants for flexibility.
g) Include comments within your test cases, explaining the purpose and expected outcome of each step.

3. Unit Testing In Python:

Unit testing involves testing individual units, or components, of your code in isolation. It helps ensure that each unit behaves correctly and as intended. Python's unit test framework provides tools and assertions to perform unit testing effectively.

4. Test Structure In Unittest:

In unit test, a test case is defined as a class that inherits from the TestCase class. Each test is defined as a method within the test case class. Let's illustrate this with an example:

```Python
import unittest

class MathOperationsTestCase(unittest.TestCase):
    def test_addition(self):
        result = add(3, 5)
        self.assertEqual(result, 8)
    def test_subtraction(self):
        result = subtract(10, 4)
        self.assertEqual(result, 6)
```

5. Test Execution In Unittest:

To execute the defined tests, use the unittest framework's TestLoader and TextTestRunner. Let's illustrate this with an example:

```Python
import unittest

# Define test cases and methods here.

if __name__ == '__main__':
    loader = unittest.TestLoader()
    suite = unittest.TestSuite()
    suite.addTests(loader.loadTestsFromTestCase(MathOperationsTestCase))
    runner = unittest.TextTestRunner()
    result = runner.run(suite)
```

6. Test assertions In The Unit Test:

Assertions in unit tests are used to compare the actual result with the expected result. They help validate test outcomes. Some commonly used assertions include:

a) `assertEqual(a, b)`: Checks if a and b are equal.
b) `assertTrue(x)`: Checks if x is true.
c) `assertFalse(x)`: Checks if x is false.
d) `assertRaises(exception, callable, *args, **kwargs)`: Checks if the given callable raises the specified exception.

7. Pytest Framework:

Pytest is another popular testing framework in Python known for its simplicity and ease of use. It provides powerful assertion features and supports writing both simple and complex test cases.

8. Pytest Execution:

To execute pytest tests, you need to follow these steps:

    a. Define your test functions or test classes using the `test_` prefix or `@pytest.mark` decorator.
    b. Run pytest in your terminal by navigating to the project directory and typing `pytest` or `pytest <filename.py>.`

Conclusion:

Writing test cases and performing unit testing are crucial steps in the software development process, ensuring code correctness and reliability. This section provided a detailed explanation of test case writing, unit testing concepts in Python, and the usage of the unit test and pytest frameworks. By mastering these techniques and following best practices, you can significantly improve the quality of your Python programs.

Chapter End Exercise

Multiple Choice Questions:

1. Which of the following is NOT a common debugging technique in Python?

    a) Print statements

    b) Documentation

    c) Reading tea leaves

    d) Error messages

2. What is the purpose of the pdb module in Python?

    a) To generate error messages

    b) To provide a command-line debugger for interactive debugging

    c) To execute Python code in parallel

    d) To optimize Python code for speed

3. Which of the following is NOT a commonly used assertion in unit testing?

    a) assertEqual()

    b) assertTrue()

    c) assertMaybe()

    d) assertFalse()

True and False:
1. **Logging is a useful debugging technique, especially in large and complex projects.**
   (True/False)

2. **Unit testing involves testing individual components or units of code in isolation.**
   (True/False)

3. **Pytest is the only testing framework available for Python.**
   (True/False)

4. **The logging module in Python is primarily used for debugging complex projects.**
   (True/False)

5. **Unit testing involves testing individual units of code in isolation to ensure their correctness.**
   (True/False)

6. **In the unit test framework, each test case is defined as a method within a test case class.**
   (True/False)

Coding Practice:
I. Write a Python function called **find_maximum** that takes a list of numbers as input and returns the maximum number in the list. Then, write test cases using the **unittest** framework to ensure that the function behaves as expected.

II. Write a Python function called **calculate_factorial** that calculates the factorial of a given non-negative integer. Then, write test cases using the **unittest** framework to ensure the correctness of the function.

Chapter 9: Real-World Applications

A. Creating A Web Application With Django:

In this section, we will explore how to create a web application using Django, a powerful Python web framework. Django provides a high-level, feature-rich environment for rapid application development.

1. Setting Up Django:

To begin, you need to have Django installed on your computer. We assume you have Python installed already. Open your terminal or command prompt and run the following command to install Django using pip, Python's package installer:

```
pip install Django
```

Once installed, you can verify the installation by running:

```
python -m django --version
```

This should display the version number if Django is successfully installed.

2. Creating A New Django Project:

To create a new Django project, open your terminal or command prompt and navigate to the desired location where you want to create the project. Then, run the following command:

```
django-admin startproject myproject
```

This will create a new directory named 'myproject' with the basic structure of a Django project.

3. Exploring Django Project Structure:

Inside the 'myproject' directory, you will find several files and directories. The 'manage.py' file is a command-line tool for managing your Django project. The 'myproject' directory contains the project settings and configurations.

4. Creating a Django App:

A Django project typically consists of one or more apps. An app represents a specific functionality or feature of the web application. To create a new app, navigate to the project directory and run the following command:

```
python manage.py startapp myapp
```

This will create a new directory named 'myapp' within your project.

5. Building Models:

Models define the structure of your data and are created using Python classes. Open the 'models.py' file inside the 'myapp' directory and define the necessary models using Django's model fields. For example, let's create a 'User' model with 'username' and 'email' fields:

```Python
from django.db import models

class User(models.Model):
    username = models.CharField(max_length=100)
    email = models.EmailField()
```

6. Migrating The Database:

After creating the models, you need to migrate the database to create the corresponding tables. Django provides a database-agnostic migration framework. Run the following command in your terminal:

```
python manage.py makemigrations
```

This command will generate the necessary database migration files based on the changes in your models. To apply these migrations and create the tables, run the following:

```
python manage.py migrate
```

7. Creating Views:

Views handle the logic and control the flow of data between models and templates. In your 'myapp' directory, open the 'views.py' file and create a view function. For example, let's define a 'home' view that fetches all the users from the database:

```Python
from django.shortcuts import render

from models import User

def home(request):
    users = User.objects.all()
    return render(request, 'home.html', {'users': users})
```

8. Designing Templates:

Templates define the structure and layout of the web pages. Create a 'templates' directory within the 'app' directory. Inside it, create an 'home.html' file with the following content:

```HTML
<!DOCTYPE html>
<html>
<head>
    <title>User List</title>
```

```
</head>
<body>
  <h1>User List</h1>
  <ul>
    {% for user in users %}
    <li>{{ user.username }} - {{ user.email }}</li>
    {% endfor %}
  </ul>
</body>
</html>
```

9. Mapping URLs:

URLs define the mapping between the URLs entered by the user and the associated views. Open the 'urls.py' file in the 'my project' directory and add the following code:

```Python
from django.urls import path
from myapp.Views import home
URL patterns = [
    path('', home, name='home'),
```

10. Testing The Web Application:

To start the development server and test your web application, run the following command:

```
python manage.py runserver
```

This will start the server at 'http://127.0.0.1:8000/'. Open this URL in your web browser to see your web application in action.

Congratulations! You have successfully created a web application using Django. This was just a basic overview; Django offers many more advanced features for building scalable and complex web applications. Explore the Django documentation for further learning and enhancement of your web development skills.

Illustrations And Examples:

Throughout this section, we have illustrated the concepts using code snippets. These examples provide a practical understanding of working with Django and building a web application step by step. Additionally, the provided HTML template and code snippets are accompanied by clear explanations to ease comprehension.

By following along with the examples and illustrations, beginners in Python programming will gain a solid foundation in creating web applications using Django. Remember to experiment and modify the code to improve your understanding and explore the possibilities Django offers.

B. Building A Data Analysis Project With Pandas And NumPy

In this section, we will explore the powerful libraries pandas and NumPy for building data analysis projects using the Python programming language. We will cover the basics of these libraries, explain their functionality, and provide illustrative examples and code snippets to reinforce your understanding.

Introduction To Pandas And NumPy:

- Pandas is a Python library that provides high-level data structures and data analysis tools. It is built on top of NumPy and is widely used in data manipulation and analysis tasks.

NumPy is a fundamental library for numerical computations in Python. It provides support for large, multi-dimensional arrays and a collection of functions to efficiently operate on these arrays.

Installing Pandas And NumPy:

Before we dive into the details, let's ensure that we have Pandas and NumPy installed. You can install them using pip or conda by executing the following commands in your terminal:

```
pip install pandas

pip install numpy
```

Importing Pandas And NumPy:

To use these libraries in your Python project, you need to import them first. Conventionally, pandas are imported as `pd,` and NumPy is imported as `np.` Add the following import statements at the top of your Python script:

```Python
import pandas as pd

import numpy as np
```

Loading And Exploring Data With Pandas:

Data analysis often begins with loading and exploring the data. Pandas provide various functions to read data from different sources, such as CSV files, Excel files, databases, etc. Let's start by loading a CSV file with pandas:

```Python
data = pd.read_csv('data.csv)
```

This will load the data from the CSV file 'data.csv' into a pandas DataFrame, a data structure that allows us to manipulate and analyze the data easily.

Once the data is loaded, we can perform various operations to explore it further. For instance, we can view the first few rows of the dataset using the `head()` function:

```python
print(data.head())
```

```

This will print the first five rows of the data frame. Similarly, the `tail()` function displays the last five rows.

**Basic Data Manipulation With Pandas:**

Pandas provides several functions and methods to manipulate and transform data. Here are a few commonly used ones:

**- Selecting columns:**

'''Python

column = data['column_name']

```

This will select a specific column from the DataFrame and assign it to the variable' column.'

- Filtering rows:

'''Python

filtered_data = data[data['column_name'] > 100]

```

This will filter the data based on a specific condition and assign the filtered data to the variable' filtered_data.'

**- Sorting data:**

'''Python

sorted_data = data.sort_values(by='column_name', ascending=False)
```

```

This will sort the data based on a specific column in descending order.

### Performing Numerical Computations With NumPy:

Now, let's explore some basic numerical computations using NumPy.

### - Creating Arrays:

```Python

arr = np.array([1, 2, 3, 4, 5])

```

This will create a NumPy array containing the specified elements.

- Performing Mathematical Operations:

```Python

result = np.add(arr, 10)

print(result) # Output [11 12 13 14 15]

```

This will add 10 to each element in the array 'arr' and store the result in the variable 'result.'

- Statistical Computations:

```Python

mean = np.mean(arr)

```
std = np.std(arr)
```

This will calculate the mean and standard deviation of the array 'arr.'

Conclusion:

In this section, you learned how to build a data analysis project using pandas and NumPy. We covered the basics of these libraries, explained their functionality, and provided illustrative examples and code snippets. Armed with this knowledge, you can now start exploring the world of data analysis using Python.

C. Developing A Game Using The Pygame Library:
Introduction:

In this section, we will explore the exciting world of game development using the Python programming language. Specifically, we will focus on the Pygame library, a powerful framework that allows us to create games and multimedia applications with ease. Throughout this section, we will provide in-depth explanations, illustrative examples, and helpful illustrations to guide beginners on their journey to developing their games.

1. Setting Up Pygame:

Before we dive into the game development process, it's essential to set up the Pygame library on your system. Here's a step-by-step guide:

Step 1: Installing Pygame:

- Visit the official Pygame website at "www.pygame.org" and navigate to the "Downloads" section.
- Depending on your system configuration (e.g., Windows, Mac, or Linux), choose the appropriate installation file.
- Follow the installation instructions provided on the website to install Pygame on your computer.

Step 2: Importing The Pygame Library:

- Open your Python Integrated Development Environment (IDE) or text editor.

- Import the Pygame library by adding the following line of code at the beginning of your script:

```Python
import pygame
```

2. Basic Game Development Concepts:

Before we dive into building our game, it's essential to understand a few fundamental concepts:

- **Game Loop:**

A game loop handles the logic of updating the game state, processing user inputs, and rendering visuals. It typically consists of event handling, updating game entities, and rendering the scene repeatedly to provide an interactive experience.

- **Sprites:**

Sprites represent any character, object, or entity within the game. They can be static or animated, created with images, shapes, or both. Pygame provides built-in classes and functions to manipulate sprites efficiently.

• **Collision Detection:**

Collision detection is crucial in games to determine if two objects are intersecting or interacting. Pygame offers various collision detection methods and functions to handle collisions effectively.

3. Creating A Pygame Window:

To develop a game using Pygame, we need to create a window to display our game's graphics and provide a user interface. Here's an example illustrating how to create a basic Pygame window:

```Python
import pygame

# Initialize Pygame

pygame.init()

# Set the window size

window_width = 900

window_height = 700

window = pygame.display.set_mode((window_width, window_height))

# Set the window title

pygame.display.set_caption("My Amazing Game!")
```

```
# Main game loop
running = True
while running:
    # Process events
    for event in pygame.event.get():
        if event.type == pygame.QUIT:
            running = False
    # Update game logic
    # Render visuals
    window.fill((255, 255, 255))
    pygame.display.update()
# Quit Pygame
pygame.quit()
```

4. Incorporating User Input:

User input is vital for interactive games. Pygame provides various ways to handle user input, such as mouse events, keyboard events, and joystick events. Here's an example illustrating how to handle keyboard input:

```Python
# Inside the game loop
for event in pygame.event.get():
```

```
    if event.type == pygame.KEYDOWN:
        if event.key == pygame.K_LEFT:
            # Handle left arrow key press
            player.move_left()
        elif event.key == pygame.K_RIGHT:
            # Handle right arrow key press
            player.move_right()
        elif event.key == pygame.K_SPACE:
            # Handle the spacebar key press
            player.jump()
```

5. Working With Game Sprites:

Sprites play a vital role in games, as they represent various objects and characters. Pygame provides a built-in class called `pygame.sprite.Sprite` for sprite manipulation. Here's an example illustrating how to create a simple sprite:

```
Python

# Create a sprite class
class Player(pygame.sprite.Sprite):
    def __init__(self):
        super().__init__()
```

```
        # Load the player image
        self.image = pygame.image.load("player.png")
        self.rect = self.image.get_rect()
        # Set the initial position
        self.rect.x = 100
        self.rect.y = 100
    def update(self):
        # Implement sprite updates
        pass
# Inside the game loop
player = Player()
all_sprites = pygame.Sprite.Group()
all_sprites.add(player)
# Update and render all sprites
all_sprites.update()
all_sprites.draw(window)
```

6. Implementing Collision Detection:

Collision detection is pivotal in games to handle interactions between sprites efficiently. Pygame provides built-in collision detection methods such as `pygame.Sprite.Sprite collide ()` to detect collisions between sprites. Here's an example illustrating collision detection between the player and an enemy sprite:

```Python
# Inside the game loop
collisions = pygame.sprite.sprite.collide(player, enemies, True)
if collisions:
    # Handle collision between player and enemy
    player.health -= 10
```

Conclusion:

By following the examples and explanations provided in this section, beginners can start their exciting journey into game development using the Pygame library. We've covered the basics of setting up Pygame, concepts such as sprites and collision detection, and incorporating user input to create an interactive gaming experience. With further exploration and practice, you'll be able to create your very own Python games that can entertain and engage players.

Chapter End Exercise

Multiple Choice Questions:

1. **Which Python library is used for building web applications?**

    - A) NumPy
    - B) Pandas
    - C) Pygame
    - D) Django

2. **What command is used to start the development server in Django?**

    - A) python runserver
    - B) manage.py start
    - C) python manage.py runserver
    - D) start server

3. **Which library is primarily used for data manipulation and analysis in Python?**

    - A) NumPy
    - B) Pygame
    - C) Django
    - D) Pandas

4. **What function is used to load a CSV file in Pandas?**

    - A) load_csv()
    - B) read_csv()
    - C) import_csv()

- D) open_csv()

5. Which library is used for game development in Python?

- A) NumPy
- B) Pandas
- C) Django
- D) Pygame

True and False:
1. Pygame is primarily used for data analysis in Python.

    (True/False)

2. Django provides a high-level environment for the rapid development of web applications.

    (True/False)

3. NumPy is built on top of Pandas for numerical computations in Python.

    (True/False)

4. Creating a new Django project is done using the command django-admin startproject.

    (True/False)

5. Collision detection is not necessary in game development.

    (True/False)

Coding Practice:

I. Create a Django model for a **Product** with fields **name**, **price**, and **description**.

II. Load a CSV file named **data.csv** using Pandas and display the first ten rows of the DataFrame.

III. Write a Pygame script to create a window with a red background color.

IV. Implement a sprite class named **Enemy** in Pygame with an image named **enemy.png** and initial position at (200, 200).

V. Implement a Django view named **products_list** that fetches all products from the database and renders them in a template named **products.html**.

Chapter 10: Best Practices And Further Resources

A. Clean Coding Practices:

In this section, we will discuss the importance of clean coding practices and provide guidelines to help beginners improve the quality and readability of their Python code. By following these practices, you will not only write code that is easier to understand but will also save time and effort in the long run.

1. Use Meaningful Variable And Function Names:

When naming variables and functions, always choose meaningful names that accurately describe their purpose. This makes your code self-explanatory and easier to read.

For example:

```Python
# Bad:
x = 5
y = 10
z = x + y

# Good:
num1 = 5
num2 = 10
sum_values = num1 + num2
```

2. Write Clear And Concise Comments:

Comments are important for documenting your code and providing additional context to readers. However, avoid excessive commenting and ensure that your comments are concise and relevant. Over-commenting can clutter the code and make it harder to understand.

For instance:

```Python
# Bad:
# This variable stores the result of the calculation
result = 0

# Good:
Result = 0 # Stores the result of the calculation
```

3. Organize Code With Proper Indentation:

Python relies on indentation to define code blocks, so it is crucial to use consistent and proper indentation. This enhances code readability and reduces the chances of introducing errors. Here's an example of correctly indented code:

```Python
# Bad:
if(age > 18):
print("You are an adult.")
```

```
# Good:

if age > 18:

    print("You are an adult.")
```
```

### 4. Avoid Code Redundancy:

Redundant code not only increases the size of your program but also makes it difficult to maintain and debug. Look for opportunities to eliminate duplication and refactor your code. This improves efficiency and reduces the chances of introducing bugs.

**For example:**

```Python
# Bad:

if grade == "A":

    print("Excellent!")
elif grade == "A":
    print("Great job!")

# Good:

if grade == "A":

        print("Excellent!")

elif grade == "B":
```
```

```
print("Great job!")
```

5. Break Down Complex Code Into Smaller Functions:

Complex code blocks are harder to understand and debug. Whenever possible, break down complicated logic into smaller, reusable functions. This promotes code reusability, readability, and maintenance. Let's consider the following example:

```Python
# Bad:
def calculate_average(numbers):
    total = 0
    count = 0
    for num in numbers:
        total += num
        count += 1
    average = total / count
    return average

# Good:
def calculate_average(numbers):
    total = sum(numbers)
    count = len(numbers)
```

    average = total / count

    return average

```

## 6. Properly Document Your Code:

Documenting your code is essential for collaborating with others and for future reference. Follow docstring conventions to provide clear and concise descriptions for your functions, modules, and classes. This helps readers understand the purpose, arguments, and return values of your code. Consider the following example:

```Python

def calculate_average(numbers):
    """
    Calculates the average of a list of numbers.

    Parameters:
    Numbers (list): A list of numbers.

    Returns:
    Float: The average value.
    """
    total = sum(numbers)

    count = len(numbers)

    average = total / count

    return average

```

By adopting these clean coding practices, you will develop code that is easier to read, maintain, and understand. Following these guidelines from the beginning will save you time and effort throughout your programming journey and help you become a better Python programmer.

B. Code Optimization Techniques:
Introduction:

In this section, we will explore various code optimization techniques in Python programming. Code optimization is the process of improving the efficiency and performance of your code, making it run faster and consume fewer system resources. By optimizing your code, you can enhance the overall execution speed, reduce memory usage, and improve the scalability of your Python programs. This section will provide you with an in-depth understanding of the common optimization techniques used in Python, along with illustrative examples and illustrations.

1. Use Built-In Functions:

Python provides many built-in functions that are optimized for performance. Utilizing these functions can significantly enhance the execution speed and efficiency of your code. Some commonly used built-in functions for optimization include len (), min (), max (), sum (), sorted (), enumerate (), and zip (). We will discuss how to leverage these functions and their advantages with practical examples.

Example:

```Python

```python
# Computing the sum of a list using a for-loop
numbers = [1, 2, 3, 4, 5]
sum = 0
for num in numbers:
    sum += num
print("Sum using for loop:", sum)

# Computing the sum of a list using the built-in `sum()` function
numbers = [1, 2, 3, 4, 5]
sum = sum(numbers)
print("Sum using `sum()` function:", sum)
```

2. Avoid Unnecessary Computations:

Avoid performing unnecessary computations, especially within loops. Redundant calculations can significantly impact your code's performance. Analyze your code and identify sections where you can eliminate redundant computations or unnecessary iterations.

Example:

```Python
# Redundant computation within a loop
numbers = [1, 2, 3, 4, 5]
sum = 0
```

```
for num in numbers:
    sum += num * 2
print("Sum with redundant computation:", sum)
# Optimized code without redundant computation
numbers = [1, 2, 3, 4, 5]
sum = 0
multiplier = 2
for num in numbers:
    sum += num * multiplier
print("Sum without redundant computation:", sum)
```

3. List Comprehensions:

List comprehensions offer a concise and optimized way to create lists. They are more efficient compared to traditional loops, resulting in improved performance by avoiding the overhead of creating an empty list, looping, and repeatedly appending elements.

Example:

```Python
# Creating a list of squared numbers using a for-loop
numbers = [1, 2, 3, 4, 5]
squared_numbers = []
```

```
for num in numbers:

    squared_numbers.append(num ** 2)

print("Squared numbers using for loop:", squared_numbers)

# Optimized code using list comprehension

numbers = [1, 2, 3, 4, 5]

squared_numbers = [num ** 2 for num in numbers]

print("Squared numbers using list comprehension:", squared_numbers)
```

4. Avoid Unnecessary Function Calls:

Reducing the number of function calls in your code can lead to significant performance gains. Function calls introduce additional overhead, such as parameter passing and stack management. Try to optimize your code by minimizing function calls.

Example:

```Python
# Unoptimized code with unnecessary function calls

def square(num):
    return num ** 2

numbers = [1, 2, 3, 4, 5]
```

```
    squared_numbers = [square(num) for num in numbers]

    print("Squared numbers with unnecessary function calls:", squared_numbers)

    # Optimized code without unnecessary function calls

    numbers = [1, 2, 3, 4, 5]

    squared_numbers = [num ** 2 for num in numbers]

    print("Squared numbers without unnecessary function calls:", squared_numbers)
```

5. Efficient Data Structures:

Choosing the appropriate data structures can significantly impact the performance of your code. Certain data structures, such as dictionaries (`dict`), sets (`set`), and tuples (`tuple`), offer better performance for specific operations. Consider your code's requirements and select the most efficient data structure accordingly.

Example:

```Python
# Unoptimized code using a list for membership check

names = ["Alice," "Bob," "Charlie"]

if "Alice" in names:

    print("Alice found!")

# Optimized code using a set for membership check
```

```
names = {"Alice," "Bob," "Charlie"}

if "Alice" in names:

    print("Alice found!")
```
```

**Conclusion:**

In this section, we discussed various code optimization techniques in Python programming. By utilizing built-in functions, avoiding unnecessary computations, using list comprehensions, minimizing function calls, and selecting efficient data structures, you can significantly enhance the performance and efficiency of your Python code. It is essential to analyze your code, identify areas for optimization, and apply suitable techniques to achieve the desired improvements in execution speed and resource utilization.

Throughout the section, illustrations and examples have been provided to help you better understand how these techniques can be applied in practice. Experiment with these optimization techniques in your code to observe the positive impact they can have on performance.

## C. Resources For Further Learning And Community Support:
**Introduction**:

In this section, we will explore the wealth of resources available to beginners in Python programming. Learning a new programming language can be challenging, but with the right tools and support, your journey can be exciting and fruitful. We will discuss various platforms, online
```

communities, forums, and additional materials that can aid in your understanding of Python.

1. Online Learning Platforms:

a. Codecademy:

Codecademy offers interactive Python courses designed specifically for beginners. Their comprehensive curriculum covers the fundamentals, syntax, and best practices in Python programming. The platform includes hands-on exercises, quizzes, and projects to reinforce your understanding.

b. Coursera:

Coursera hosts a wide range of Python courses from reputed universities and organizations. These courses are crafted to suit beginners and also offer certified programs upon completion. Assignments, quizzes, and valuable feedback from peers and instructors accompany the interactive lessons.

2. Official Python Documentation:

The official Python documentation is a treasure trove for beginners and experienced developers alike. It provides comprehensive explanations of the Python language, built-in functions, libraries, and modules. The documentation is regularly updated and offers detailed examples and usage scenarios to help you understand Python concepts thoroughly.

3. Online Communities And Forums:

a. Stack Overflow:

Stack Overflow is a community-driven platform where programmers can ask and answer technical questions related to Python and other programming languages. It is an excellent resource for beginners encountering coding challenges or seeking guidance on specific Python topics. Ensure to search for existing queries before posting your question.

b. Reddit:

The Python community on Reddit is vibrant and welcoming to beginners. Subreddits such as r/learnpython and r/python offer a supportive environment for asking questions, sharing experiences, and discovering new learning resources.

Conclusion:

As a beginner in Python programming, leveraging the available resources and community support can greatly enhance your learning experience. Online learning platforms like Codecademy and Coursera provide structured courses, while platforms like Stack Overflow and Reddit connect you with experts and enthusiasts ready to assist. The official Python documentation serves as a comprehensive reference guide. Remember to practice regularly, ask questions, and join online communities to maximize your Python programming potential.

Chapter End Exercise

Multiple Choice Questions (MCQs):

1. **Which of the following is a clean coding practice in Python?**

a) Using arbitrary variable names

b) Over-commenting to provide extensive context

c) Indenting code inconsistently

d) Using meaningful variable and function names

2. **What is the purpose of code optimization in Python?**

a) To make the code less readable

b) To increase the number of lines in the code

c) To improve efficiency and performance

d) To introduce more redundancy in the code

3. **Which built-in function is optimized for computing the sum of a list in Python?**

a) total()

b) add()

c) sum()

d) compute_sum()

4. **Which of the following is a benefit of using list comprehensions in Python?**

a) They make the code longer and harder to read

b) They introduce redundancy in the code

c) They are less efficient compared to traditional loops

d) They provide a concise and optimized way to create lists

5. **Which data structure is more efficient for membership check operations in Python?**

a) List

b) Dictionary

c) Tuple

d) Set

True/False:

1. Proper indentation is not necessary in Python as long as the code executes correctly.

    (True/False)

2. List comprehensions are less efficient compared to traditional loops in Python.

    (True/False)

3. Avoiding unnecessary function calls can lead to performance gains in Python.

    (True/False)

4. Reddit is not a suitable platform for beginners to seek support and resources for Python programming.

    (True/False)

5. Using meaningful variable and function names is not essential for writing clean code in Python.

    (True/False)

Coding Practice:

1. Write a Python function called **remove_duplicates** that takes a list as input and returns a new list with duplicate elements removed.

2. Implement a Python script that calculates the factorial of a given number using recursion.

3. Write a Python program that prompts the user to enter a list of numbers, then computes and prints the sum of all the even numbers in the list.

4. Create a Python function called **find_common_elements** that takes two lists as input and returns a new list containing the common elements between the two input lists.

5. Develop a Python script that reads a text file and counts the frequency of each word in the file, then prints the word-frequency pairs sorted by frequency in descending order.

www.ingramcontent.com/pod-product-compliance
Lightning Source LLC
Chambersburg PA
CBHW052148220526
45471CB00004B/1581